OUR HOLY FAITH

BOOK FOUR

BREAD OF LIFE

TAN Books
Gastonia, North Carolina

Originally published in 1961 as *Our Holy Faith Book IV: The Vine and the Branches* by Bruce Publishing Company and reprinted in 1998 by The Neumann Press.

Nihil Obstat:
John F. Murphy, S.T.D.
Censor Librorum
Imprimatur:
William E. Cousins
Archbishop of Milwaukee
March 13, 1961

This TAN Books edition has been re-typeset and enhanced with additional content and revisions, including modernized language and updates to the practices of the Catholic Church. Catechism questions and answers have been replaced with the TAN edition of *The Third Council of Baltimore: Baltimore Catechism 1–4.*

Scripture quotes are adapted from the Douay-Rheims 1899 American Edition.

Content revisions and updates by Elisa Torres
Interior design by Caroline Green
Cover design by www.davidferrisdesign.com

ISBN: 978-1-5051-1923-7

Published in the United States by
TAN Books
PO Box 269
Gastonia, NC 28053
www.TANBooks.com
Printed in the United States of America

Contents

Publisher's Note

The original editions of the *Our Holy Faith* series textbooks were published between 1959 and 1964. They were compiled by many different authors over the course of several years. Consequently, the texts varied in their organization from year to year, with similar sections appearing with different names throughout the series and often in varying sequences.

For greater ease of use and consistency, we have reorganized each book so that the Catechism lessons, tests, and other exercises are placed at the end of each relevant chapter or lesson. We have also included answer keys for your convenience in the back of each book.

While the teachings in the original editions remain relevant due to the enduring truths of our Faith, it was necessary to update other aspects in order to more accurately reflect the Church today. These new editions have been revised to incorporate some of the changes to the practices of the Catholic Church.

To the extent possible, we have adapted the text to reflect both the ordinary and extraordinary forms of the Mass and liturgical calendars. In addition to these updates, we have inserted, where relevant to the text, traditional prayers and quotes from the Bible, the Catechism, and the saints.

This new Our Holy Faith series is faithful to the work of the original authors. It honors the fundamental and unchanging truths of the Catholic Church and is heavily influenced by tradition. We believe it is the catechesis you can trust with your children's faith.

UNIT

1 What We Believe

The things that we believe help us to live the life of a Christian. In the four chapters of unit 1 we shall review the most important truths we believe. Then we shall begin our special work of this year.

Our big task in the fourth grade is to learn how the Church has arranged the whole year to help us live these truths of our Holy Faith by re-living the life of Christ with our Blessed Redeemer in the seasons and feasts of the Church Year.

Everything that we shall review in this first unit will help us learn how to follow the liturgy, and will help us to live with, in, and through Christ during the Church Year.

CHAPTER 1

God the Father: Creation and Fall of Man

> *"I believe in God, the Father Almighty, Creator of heaven and earth. . . ."*

God and His Perfections

Last year we learned that God is the Creator of heaven and earth. God alone had no beginning. No one made Him. He lives from all eternity. He always was and He always will be. God is *eternal.*

God needs no one. He depends upon no one for anything. Since He is above every created thing, we call Him the *Supreme Being.* He is all that is true, all that is good, all that is beautiful. He is powerful and wise. He knows all things—past, present, and future. He knows our deepest secrets. There is nothing that we can hide from God. He is *all-knowing.* He is everywhere. He is *all-present.*

Because God is *all-good* as well as *almighty* and *all-wise,* He created the world. He made the world out of nothing. We can make an airplane, a wagon, or a doll dress if we have the materials on hand. We cannot make any of these things if we have no supplies. A man can build a house; but he needs wood, bricks, and other things to make the house. He cannot build a house

from nothing. God, however, can make things from nothing, and for this reason we say *God is the Creator of heaven and earth and of all things.*

Why God Made Man

Do you remember the wonderful story of the creation? How did God make the first man? He formed man's body from the dust of the earth and gave it a soul. The soul is immortal. It will never die. God made man to His own image and likeness. Therefore, *man is a creature composed of body and soul and made in the image and likeness of God.* By "man" we mean every human being—you and me and all people.

God created man to show forth His goodness. He made man to be happy with Him in heaven.

By creating us, God shared His goodness with us. He gave us minds to know Him, hearts to love Him, and free wills to choose Him and put our trust in Him.

To become holy and to be happy with God in this world and forever in heaven we must *know, love, and serve* Him. By knowing, loving, and serving God in this life, we fulfill His will and begin to enjoy a taste of the joys of heaven. God wants to give us Himself today, but He will do so only if we open our hearts to His presence. Through the Catholic Church, God teaches us what we must know and do in order to be faithful to the Church's teachings. Through the Holy Sacrifice of the Mass, the sacraments, and prayer, God gives us the grace to do all that He wants us to do. The saints, too, by their holy example teach us how to know, love, and serve God. God has also given us certain laws or rules to follow. These laws are like signposts along the road to heaven, showing us the way to the home of our heavenly Father. Some of these laws are the *Ten Commandments.* Do you remember them? They were given to us by God on Mount Sinai. If we really love God, we will keep His commandments. By being faithful to the laws and teachings of the Church, we can better understand the unique plan God has for each of us.

> *Not every one that says to me, Lord, Lord, shall enter into the kingdom of heaven: but he that does the will of my Father who is in heaven, he shall enter into the kingdom of heaven.*
>
> *—Matthew 7:21*

The Fall of Man

When God placed Adam and Eve in the beautiful Garden of Eden, they were completely happy. Nobody on earth has ever been so happy as they were. There was no pain or sorrow. God gave our first parents everything; the whole world was theirs. Above all, God adopted them as His children and gave them a share in His divine life. They received a special supernatural gift that made them holy and pleasing to God. This gift was *sanctifying grace.*

They knew that they would remain happy as long as they served God. They were to pass their happiness on to all the people who came after them. However, Adam and Eve's perfect harmony with God was put to the test. The Bible tells us a story to help us understand.

In the Garden of Eden there were many trees. God told our first parents that they could eat the fruit from these trees. There was one tree, however, whose fruit God forbade them to eat. This tree was called the tree "of the knowledge of good and evil" (Gen. 2:17). Adam and Eve, influenced by the cunning serpent, took the forbidden fruit and ate of it. After Adam and Eve disobeyed God, sin, suffering, sadness, evil, and death came into the world. Worst of all, they lost sanctifying grace. God stopped dwelling perfectly in their souls, and the gates of heaven were closed. Adam, as the head of the human race, was told that he would have to work hard for the rest of his life. Eve, too, was punished. What did God tell her?

The Promise of a Redeemer

God sent our first parents out of the Garden of Eden into a world of pain, hard work, and death; but He did not stop loving them because they had disobeyed Him. He promised to send a Redeemer who would save the world.

Satan received his punishment, too. God said that the power of Satan would be broken by a Child born of a woman. He said to the devil: "I will put enmities between you and the woman, between your seed and her seed: she shall crush your head . . ." (Gen. 3:15).

God made His promise to send a Redeemer to Adam and Eve. He repeated this promise to many holy men and women who lived long before Christ was born.

Abraham

Many years after the flood, God repeated the promise of a Messiah. This time He spoke to a man who always kept His laws. Do you remember how God tested Abraham's love? How did Abraham prove that he loved God more than he did his son, Isaac?

God tested Abraham and found that he was faithful. God said: "And I will make of you a great nation, and I will bless you, and magnify your name. . . . in you shall all the kindred of the earth be blessed" (Gen. 12:2–3).

What did God mean when He said: "In you shall all the nations of the earth be blessed"?

Jacob

It was not time for Christ to come yet. The world was not ready for the Messiah. God continued His preparation for the coming of His Son. Evil had to be overcome, and belief in the one true God had to be made stronger. Again and again, God reminded His people that a Redeemer would come.

One night when Jacob was running away from his angry brother, Esau, he stopped to rest. During his sleep, he saw a ladder reaching from earth to heaven. Angels were going up and down the ladder, and on the very top step stood the Lord Himself. He spoke to Jacob thus: "I am the Lord God of Abraham your father, and the God of Isaac; the land, wherein you sleep, I will give to you and to your seed" (Gen. 28:13–14). Again the wonderful promise of a Redeemer was given. God said: ". . . in you and your seed all the tribes of the earth shall be blessed" (Gen. 28:14).

Jacob lived to be a very old man. Shortly before his death, Jacob blessed his twelve sons. At this time he told Judah that the promised Redeemer would come from his family. "The sceptre shall not be taken away from Judah . . . till he come that is to be sent, and he shall be the expectation of nations" (Gen. 49:10).

David

David, a just and holy man, was chosen by God to be the King of Israel. While he ruled his people David sought to bring them back to God. God was very pleased with this work. He rewarded David by promising him that the Redeemer would come from his descendants. "And when your days shall be fulfilled and you sleep with your fathers, I will raise up your seed after you . . . and I will establish his kingdom" (2 Sam. 7:12, 13).

FOR ME TO REVIEW

Catechism Lesson

1. **Q. Who made the world?**
   A. God made the world.

2. **Q. Who is God?**
   A. God is the Creator of heaven and earth, and of all things.

6. **Q. Why did God make you?**
   A. God made me to know Him, to love Him, and to serve Him in this world, and to be happy with Him forever in the next.

9. **Q. What must we do to be saved?**
   A. To be saved we must worship God by faith, hope, and charity; that is, we must believe in Him, hope in Him, and love Him with all our heart.

10. **Q. How shall we know the things which we are to believe?**
   A. We shall know the things which we are to believe from the Catholic Church, through which God speaks to us.

13. **Q. What is God?**
   A. God is a spirit infinitely perfect.

14. **Q. Does God have a beginning?**
   A. God has no beginning; He always was and He always will be.

18. **Q. Does God know all things?**
   A. God knows all things, even our most secret thoughts, words, and actions.

16. **Q. If God is everywhere, why do we not see Him?**
   A. We do not see God, because He is a pure spirit and cannot be seen with bodily eyes.

17. **Q. Does God see us?**
A. God sees us and watches over us.

19. **Q. Can God do all things?**
A. God can do all things, and nothing is hard or impossible to Him.

32. **Q. Who created heaven and earth, and all things?**
A. God created heaven and earth, and all things.

3. **Q. What is man?**
A. Man is a creature composed of body and soul, and made in the image and likeness of God.

39. **Q. Who were the first man and woman?**
A. The first man and woman were Adam and Eve.

41. **Q. Did God give any command to Adam and Eve?**
A. To test their obedience God commanded Adam and Eve not to eat of a certain fruit which grew in the garden of Paradise.

43. **Q. Did Adam and Eve remain faithful to God?**
A. Adam and Eve did not remain faithful to God; but broke His command by eating the forbidden fruit.

44. **Q. What befell Adam and Eve on account of their sin?**
A. Adam and Eve, on account of their sin, lost innocence and holiness, and were doomed to sickness and death.

60. **Q. Did God abandon man after he fell into sin?**
A. God did not abandon man after he fell into sin, but promised him a Redeemer, Who was to satisfy for man's sin and reopen to him the gates of heaven.

313. **Q. What are the commandments of God?**
A. The commandments of God are these ten:

1. I am the Lord thy God, who brought thee out of the land of Egypt, out of the house of bondage. Thou

shalt not have strange gods before Me. Thou shalt not make to thyself a graven thing, nor the likeness of anything that is in heaven above, or in the earth beneath, nor of those things that are in the waters under the earth. Thou shalt not adore them, nor serve them.

2. Thou shalt not take the name of the Lord thy God in vain.
3. Remember thou keep holy the Sabbath day.
4. Honor thy father and thy mother.
5. Thou shalt not kill.
6. Thou shalt not commit adultery.
7. Thou shalt not steal.
8. Thou shalt not bear false witness against thy neighbor.
9. Thou shalt not covet thy neighbor's wife.
10. Thou shalt not covet thy neighbor's goods.

Questions

1. Who created the world?
2. Who is God?
3. What are some of the perfections of God?
4. What is man?
5. Why did God make us?
6. Who were the first man and woman?
7. How did God punish our first parents for their sin of disobedience?

FOR ME TO REMEMBER

1. God is the Creator of heaven and earth, and of all things.
2. God is the Supreme Being. He is eternal, all-knowing, all-present, all-good, almighty, and all-wise.
3. Man is composed of body and soul.
4. Man was created to the image and likeness of God.
5. Man was created for heaven.
6. Adam and Eve were the first man and woman.
7. Grace is a supernatural gift of God which makes us children of God and helps us to save our soul.
8. God promised to send a Redeemer who would save the world.

FOR ME TO DO

1. Discuss how God showed His goodness, power, and wisdom in creating the world.
2. Draw a map showing the creation of the world.
3. Learn the poem "The Wonderful World."
4. Compose a prayer in which you ask God to give you the grace to know, love, and serve Him better.
5. Read or tell the story of Moses and the Ten Commandments.
6. When God sent our first parents out of Eden, He said to Adam: "Dust thou art and unto dust thou shalt return." When do we hear the priest use these words? Of what do they remind us?

God Be in My Head

God be in my head and in my understanding. God be in my eyes and in my looking. God be in my mouth and in my speaking. God by in my heart and in my thinking. God be at my end and my departing.

CHAPTER 2

God's Plan for Fallen Man

> *"I believe . . . in Jesus Christ, His only Son, our Lord; who was conceived by the Holy Spirit, born of the Virgin Mary . . ."*

God had promised that the Redeemer would come one day. God kept His promise! God the Father sent His Son to earth to become man and to be our Savior. Jesus came down to earth to suffer and to die for us. He chose the Blessed Virgin Mary to be His Mother and was born a tiny baby. The things that He said and did are so wonderful that we want to remember them. He showed us how to live so that some day we can be in heaven with Him.

God Shows His Love and Mercy

Because Adam disobeyed God, he was driven out of the Garden of Eden. He lost sanctifying grace and became cut off from heaven. Though he had to suffer for his sin, he still hoped that God would give him another chance. What could be done to make things right between God and man? Only God could repair

the damage our first parents caused by their sin. Only God's love for man, His creature, could lead Him to make a wonderful plan for redeeming men from sin and restoring them to grace.

Let us recall how serious Adam's sin was and what really had to be done about it! Because man committed a sin against God, only God could make up for the sin. Because man had committed the sin, it was fitting, too, that man should have a part to play in his redemption. Jesus Christ is both human and divine. Jesus Christ, the God-Man, took the blame for our sins. He suffered and died for us. Christ's death restored us to God's friendship and regained the grace Adam's sin had lost. We are free to enter heaven if we do what God tells us: if we believe in His Son, Jesus, and do as He taught.

Waiting for the Savior

Now let us review how God the Son came to live on earth. Think of the many things He did and what He told us about heaven and His Father. What could have been greater than His sufferings and death for Adam's sin and ours? The graces from Calvary were not a one time event. Today He is still helping us through the Catholic Church, which guides us on the way to heaven.

Before Jesus came into the world there were many holy men called *prophets* who foretold His coming. The last of these was St. John the Baptist. He prepared the people for Jesus by telling them to get their hearts ready. He told them to be sorry for their sins and to do penance for them.

Do you remember how Jesus came to the River Jordan? What happened there? The Holy Spirit came upon Jesus in the form of a dove and the Father said: "This is my beloved Son, in whom I am well pleased" (Mt. 3:17).

It is well to think over the wonderful years that Jesus spent here on earth. By coming to live with us, He offered God such glory, love, obedience, and suffering that He more than made up for the sin of our first parents. In doing so, He also showed us how He wants us to live!

The Life of Our Savior

The life of our Savior is the greatest story ever told! We hear parts of it year after year. This year as we go through it again we will try to live with Christ in the way that the Church shows us—through the liturgical year and the Church's feast days. Let us recall the main events.

Annunciation

How well do you remember the story of the angel's visit to Mary? Our Lady was alone. Her soul was full of love for God. What message could have been more wonderful than that of the Angel Gabriel to Mary? The angel *announces* to her that she will bear a son, Jesus. Because she had said yes to God's will, the Son of God became man, and He began to live among us as our Savior.

> *"The Virgin did not merely pronounce her fiat; in every moment she fulfilled that firm and irrevocable decision. So should we."*
>
> *—St. Josemaria Escriva*

Visitation

Our Blessed Lady then went to her cousin, St. Elizabeth. At once Elizabeth knew of the great thing that had happened to Mary, she knew she was being *visited* by Jesus. Then Mary praised God by a beautiful prayer called the "Magnificat." At this time, too, John the Baptist was blessed in a special way.

Nativity

Finally, the first great Christmas Day came and our Savior was born! Can you tell the story without forgetting a single part? At this great moment Jesus was born to suffer and die for our sins so that we might have eternal life.

Presentation

Forty days later our Blessed Mother and St. Joseph took Jesus to *present* Him at the Temple at Jerusalem. There He offered Himself through His parents to God for our sins. Who held Jesus in his arms? What important words did he speak on this day?

Life at Nazareth

You and I would have liked to live with Christ those thirty years when He stayed with His Blessed Mother and St. Joseph at Nazareth. Every word He said, every step He took, would have helped us to do right. Jesus obeyed St. Joseph with great respect and love. He always helped His Mother. We would have liked Jesus because He was so good and kind and helpful, but would we have known that He was God the Son? It was a great secret!

Public Life

We all know that the public life of Jesus was not long. It lasted only three years. Do you remember how Jesus preached about God's kingdom through stories, and how He taught men to be sorry for their sins, to love God, and to love their neighbor, and even their enemies? Jesus also performed many miracles, like healing the deaf and blind and raising Lazarus from the dead.

We believe that all Jesus said is true because Jesus is God. He is Truth. We hope to get to heaven some day because our Redeemer won it back for us.

Passion and Death

Jesus showed His great love for us by His life and, in a very special way, by His Passion and death.

Let us recall the events of Holy Week. What happened during those important days? We follow Jesus sorrowfully from Palm Sunday, the day He rode through the streets of Jerusalem, until Good Friday when He gave up His life on Calvary so that we might regain God's great and loving friendship.

Resurrection and Ascension

On Easter Sunday, when He rose from the dead, Christ gave us the greatest proof that He is God. His life, all His sufferings and death, meant something now. He defeated sin and death. He was victorious! Now that His work was done, He was going back to heaven, where He would prepare a place for us.

The Apostles were blessed to be so close to our Savior! He made St. Peter the first pope of His Church. He made the other Apostles bishops. He told them to wait for the Holy Spirit, whom He would send to remind them of all the things that He had taught them. He was also going to teach them all the things that they would have to know. Jesus promised to stay with the Apostles and their successors forever by sending the Holy Spirit. He said to them: "I am with you all days, even to the consummation of the world" (Mt. 28:20).

"And they found the stone rolled back from the sepulchre. And going in, they found not the body of the Lord Jesus."
—Luke 24:2–3

FOR ME TO REVIEW

Catechism Lesson

61. Q. Who is the Redeemer?
A. Our Blessed Lord and Savior Jesus Christ is the Redeemer of mankind.

62. Q. Who is Jesus Christ?
A. Jesus Christ is the Son of God, the second Person of the Blessed Trinity, true God and true man.

Questions

1. Who is Jesus Christ?
2. How did Jesus make up for the sin of Adam and Eve?
3. What is a prophet?
4. How did St. John the Baptist prepare the people for the coming of Christ?
5. Name some of the chief events in the life of Christ.
6. What did Christ prove by His resurrection?
7. Who was the first pope?

FOR ME TO REMEMBER

1. Holy men who foretold the coming of Jesus were called prophets.
2. Jesus Christ is true God and true Man.
3. St. John the Baptist prepared the people for Christ's coming by preaching sorrow for sin and conversion.
4. St. John the Baptist was the last prophet.
5. The Resurrection of Christ proved that He was God.

FOR ME TO DO

1. Read the Bible story, in the book of Genesis, about the Fall of Adam and Eve; list the punishments found in the story.
2. Explain how sin brought Jesus to earth.
3. List some of the wonderful things that happened because Jesus suffered and died for us.

4. Write the great words God the Father said over His divine Son at the River Jordan.

5. Draw one of these events:

   Annunciation
   Presentation
   Nativity
   Resurrection

CHAPTER 3
The Holy Spirit and the Church

> *"I believe in the Holy Spirit,*
> *the Holy Catholic Church . . ."*

Coming of the Holy Spirit

Christ remained on earth forty days after His Resurrection. During this time, He continued to teach His Apostles. He gave them many proofs of His love. At last, He promised them that He would return to His Father and would send them the Holy Spirit, who would teach them all things.

After Christ ascended into heaven, the Apostles gathered in an upper room. Here they remained in prayer for nine days. On the tenth day a sound like a mighty wind filled the house, and tongues of fire came down on all present. They were filled with the Holy Spirit.

The Apostles, who were afraid of the Jews since Christ's death on the cross, were now brave and fearless. Filled with the Holy Spirit, St. Peter preached about Jesus crucified, and all the Apostles spoke about the wonderful works of God. Among the people who heard them were many strangers visiting in Jerusalem. Since they came from different countries, they spoke different languages, but miraculously understood everything that the Apostles were saying! This was called the gift of tongues,

a very special gift that the Holy Spirit gave the Apostles on the feast of Pentecost. As a result, about three thousand people were baptized.

The Birthday of the Church

The feast of Pentecost is called "The Birthday of the Catholic Church" because this is when the Church began, as the Apostles proclaimed the Gospel to all people. Christ promised His Apostles that the Holy Spirit would remain with the Church forever, to teach its members and to make them holy. The Holy Spirit's work will continue until the end of the world through the teaching of the pope, the bishops, and the priests of the Catholic Church.

Do you know the name of the present pope? Who is our bishop? What is your pastor's name?

FOR ME TO REVIEW

Questions

1. When did the Holy Spirit come down upon the Apostles?
2. What happened to the Apostles after the Holy Spirit came down upon them?
3. When do we celebrate the birthday of the Church?

FOR ME TO REMEMBER

1. On Pentecost the Holy Spirit came upon the Apostles in the form of fiery tongues.
2. Pentecost marks the beginning of the Catholic Church on earth.
3. The work of the Holy Spirit is carried on by the pope, the bishops, the priests, the religious brothers and sisters, and all true Christians.

FOR ME TO DO

1. Tell the story of the first Pentecost in your own words.
2. Learn the hymn: "Come, Holy Ghost."

Come, Holy Ghost

Come, Holy Ghost, fill the hearts of Thy faithful and kindle in them the fire of Thy love.

V. Send forth Thy Spirit and they shall be created;
R. And Thou shalt renew the face of the earth.

Let us pray.

O God, who didst teach the hearts of Thy faithful people by sending them the light of Thy Holy Spirit, grant us by the same Spirit to have a right judgment in all things, and evermore to rejoice in His holy comfort. Through Christ our Lord.

CHAPTER 4

The Church Leads Us to Life Everlasting

> *"I believe in . . . the*
> *communion of saints,*
> *the forgiveness of sins,*
> *the resurrection of the body,*
> *and life everlasting. Amen."*

The Communion of Saints

All of us belong to a family. Some of us belong to a large family, others to a small one. In our families, we work together, we eat together, we pray together and we share many things. In other words, we do things in common and serve each other.

In the Christ's Church, we are united with all those who are joined by grace and faith to Jesus Christ. We, the faithful on earth, the saints in heaven, and the holy souls in purgatory form the "communion of saints."

The word "communion" means a *sharing* or a *union.* And the word "saints" includes not only those who are already happy in heaven with God, but also those who are joined to Christ by baptism and faith.

So, *by "the communion of saints" is meant the union of the*

faithful on earth, the blessed in heaven, and the souls in purgatory with Christ as their Head.

The faithful on earth should honor the saints and ask them for the graces necessary to obtain the happiness of heaven. We can also help free the souls from purgatory by prayers, good works, and sacrifices, especially by the Holy Sacrifice of the Mass. Then, too, every time we recite, for example, the Prayer before a Crucifix after receiving Holy Communion, or whenever we say the Rosary, especially in the presence of the Blessed Sacrament, we can bring aid to suffering souls.

The saints in heaven intercede for us, thus assisting us to become united to them as brothers and sisters in heaven. The saints also help the souls in purgatory by praying for them.

The faithful on earth as members of the Mystical Body of Christ can help each other in many ways. Can you name some ways?

The Forgiveness of Sins

Before Jesus ascended into heaven on Ascension Day, He gave the Apostles many gifts. Do you remember any of them? What gift did He give the Apostles on Easter night? Christ appeared to the Apostles and gave them one of His great gifts, the power to forgive sins. He said to them, "Whose sins you shall forgive, they are forgiven them; and whose sins you shall retain, they are retained" (Jn. 20:23). Today, this same wonderful power is given to all priests, who are the successors of the first apostles

At Baptism, we become God's own children, free from all stain of original sin. As we grow older, we can soil our souls with sins. Some are venial sins. Others may be mortal sins, which rob us of sanctifying grace. If we commit mortal sin, the Church urgently calls upon us to seek forgiveness of our sins and to make peace with God; we know we can receive this forgiveness in the sacrament of Penance and Reconciliation, which allows us to receive the forgiveness of Christ through the priestly ministers of His Church. Remember, three things are necessary for a fruitful confession:

1. to be truly sorry for our sins,
2. to make up our minds never to sin again,
3. and to confess our sins to the priest.

If we do, we are ready to continue on our journey to heaven, filled with grace, God's own life.

The Resurrection and Life Everlasting

Did you ever wonder what happens to insects in winter? All summer long we are bothered by different kinds of flies and insects; but as soon as the cold weather sets in, there are no insects around. What happens to them?

Science books teach us that some insects hide in warm places, some live in cocoons, but most of them die.

For example, let us take the case of a caterpillar. Have you ever had a chance to watch one carefully? As soon as the colder days of the early autumn approach, the caterpillar begins to spin some fine, silky threads into a cocoon. Therein it rests during the cold winter days. It neither eats nor drinks; it doesn't work or move about. It lies quietly as though it were dead. But as soon as the warm days of spring set in, the flowers and trees begin to burst into buds, and life begins to stir in the cocoon. The covering splits open, and instead of a caterpillar a beautiful, many-colored butterfly comes forth.

Similarly, our bodies will rise from the graves at the end of the world, just as Christ rose from the dead on Easter Day. Christ promised us that when He said: "And they who have done good shall come forth unto resurrection of life; but they who have done evil unto resurrection of judgment" (Jn. 5:29).

The bodies of all men, good and bad, will rise from the dead and be reunited with their souls. They will be immortal; they will live forever. The bodies of the good will become beautiful and perfect. The bodies of the bad will become ugly. The good and holy shall enjoy God face to face. The wicked shall be punished forever.

To the good Christ will say: "Come, blessed of my Father, take possession of the kingdom prepared for you from the foundation of the world" (Mt. 25:34–35). However, Christ will turn to the wicked and say, "Depart from me, accursed ones, into the everlasting fire which was prepared for the devil and his angels" (Mt. 25: 41–42). This can be a hard truth to accept, that some will not go to heaven, but perish. God does not wish that any of His Children receive eternal punishment, but neither will He *force* anyone to cooperate with the freely-offered grace that leads souls to heaven. These then are the chief truths the Church teaches us and we profess in the Apostles' Creed. We must believe them. And we must also live these truths. Our study the rest of the year will show us what that means.

FOR ME TO REVIEW

Catechism Lesson

338. Q. What does the communion of saints mean?

A. The communion of saints means the union which exists between the members of the Church on earth with one another, and with the blessed in heaven and with the suffering souls in purgatory.

190. Q. How do the priests of the Church exercise the power of forgiving sins?

A. The priests of the Church exercise the power of forgiving sins by hearing the confession of sins, and granting pardon for them as ministers of God and in His Name.

417. Q. Will our bodies share in the reward or punishment of our souls?

A. Our bodies will share in the reward or punishment of our souls, because through the resurrection they will again be united to them.

Questions

1. Who belong to "the communion of saints"?
2. Explain the meaning of "communion" and "saints" as used in this connection.
3. How can the faithful on earth help one another?
4. What can we do to help the souls in purgatory?
5. How can the saints help us?
6. When did Christ institute the sacrament of Penance and Reconciliation?
7. How often should we receive the sacrament of Penance and Reconciliation?
8. What do we mean by "the resurrection of the body"?
9. Why will the bodies of men rise at the end of the world?
10. What is heaven?
11. What is hell?
12. What is purgatory?

FOR ME TO REMEMBER

1. The word "communion" means sharing or union.
2. In "the communion of saints" the word *saints* includes the faithful on earth, the saints in heaven, and the souls in purgatory.

3. We can help each other by prayer.
4. Christ instituted the sacrament of Penance and Reconciliation on Easter night.
5. All men will rise from the dead at the end of the world. The good shall be rewarded and the wicked shall be punished.

FOR ME TO DO

1. Draw a picture showing the three groups that belong to the "communion of saints."
2. Write a short quiz based on this chapter.
3. Make a list showing ways you can help other souls.
4. Explain how the life cycle of a butterfly is similar to the resurrection of Christ, and our own resurrection.
5. Recite the "Act of Contrition" often—especially in the morning and before going to bed.
6. Compose a prayer in which you ask the saints to obtain a special favor for you.
7. Make a small shrine for your favorite saint.

Summary of Unit 1

God, the Supreme Being, is the Creator of heaven and earth and of all things. God made man in His own image and likeness. He made man to be happy with Him in heaven. To reach heaven, we must know, love, and serve God in this world. The Catholic Church teaches us how to do this.

Adam and Eve were the first man and woman. They were blessed by God. They received from Him even a share in His own divine life. They were to pass this on to all their descendants. But, when they disobeyed God's commandment for them, Adam and Eve fell into sin. They thereby lost divine life both for themselves and for all men.

Still, God continued to love man. He promised to send His Son to atone for Adam's sin. He took under His protection a chosen people, the Hebrews, from whom the Savior was to come.

Finally, Christ, the promised Redeemer, was born in Bethlehem. He lived, suffered, and died on the cross for us. Now, reigning in glory in heaven, He still teaches us through His Mystical Body, the Church. This is made up of the faithful on earth, the poor souls in purgatory, and the saints in heaven. On earth Christ's representative is the pope, the successor of St. Peter.

Write your answers on a separate sheet of paper

Part 1 Completion

Complete the following sentences to make them correct. Use the words below to help you.

love	sharing or union	love
Catholic Church	Resurrection	St. John the Baptist
serve	Easter Day	know
eternal	Redeemer	immortal
St. Peter	communion of saints	Creator
disobeyed	sanctifying grace	
body	soul	

1. Man is a creature made up of. . . . . . and. . . . . . .
2. The soul of man is. . . . . . ; it will never die.
3. God created us to. . . . . . ,. . . . . . and. . . . . . Him in this world.
4. Because God loved man, He promised to send a. . . . . . .
5. The supernatural gift that makes men holy and pleasing to God is called. . . . . . .
6. Adam was driven out of the Garden of Eden because he. . . . . . God.
7. God is the. . . . . . because He made all things out of nothing.
8. God always was and always will be; God is. . . . . . .
9. God teaches us what we must *know* and *do* through the. . . . . . .
10. The last prophet who spoke about the coming of Christ was. . . . . . .
11. By his. . . . . . Jesus proved that He was God.
12. . . . . . . was the first pope of the Catholic Church.
13. The faithful on earth, the saints in heaven, and the souls in purgatory form the. . . . . . .
14. By "communion" we mean. . . . . . .
15. Christ gave the Apostles power to forgive sins on. . . . . . .

Part II Yes or No

Answer yes or no.

1. Were there any human beings in the world before Adam and Eve?
2. Did Adam and Eve remain faithful to God?
3. Did God punish Adam and Eve for their sin?
4. Were Adam and Eve promised a Redeemer?
5. Did God ever foretell His promise of a Redeemer?
6. Is Jesus Christ true God and true Man?
7. By His resurrection did Jesus prove that He was God?
8. Was St. John the Baptist appointed head of the Catholic Church?
9. Did Christ promise to remain with the Church forever?
10. Is Christ with the Church now?
11. Will all bodies rise at the end of the world?
12. Can the souls in purgatory help themselves by prayer?

Part 3 Arranging in Order

The names in Group A and the events in Group B are not in the correct order. Number them in the right order.

GROUP A

( ) Jacob
( ) Adam
( ) Abraham
( ) David
( ) Juda

GROUP B

( ) Ascension
( ) Nativity
( ) Passion and Death
( ) Visitation
( ) Resurrection
( ) Annunciation
( ) Presentation
( ) Pentecost

SECVND
VM·MAT
LIBER
GENERA
TIONIS
INITIV
EVANGE
LII IESV
CHRIST
SECVN
DVM
LVCAM
FVIT·
IN·DIE
HERO
DIS RE
GIS

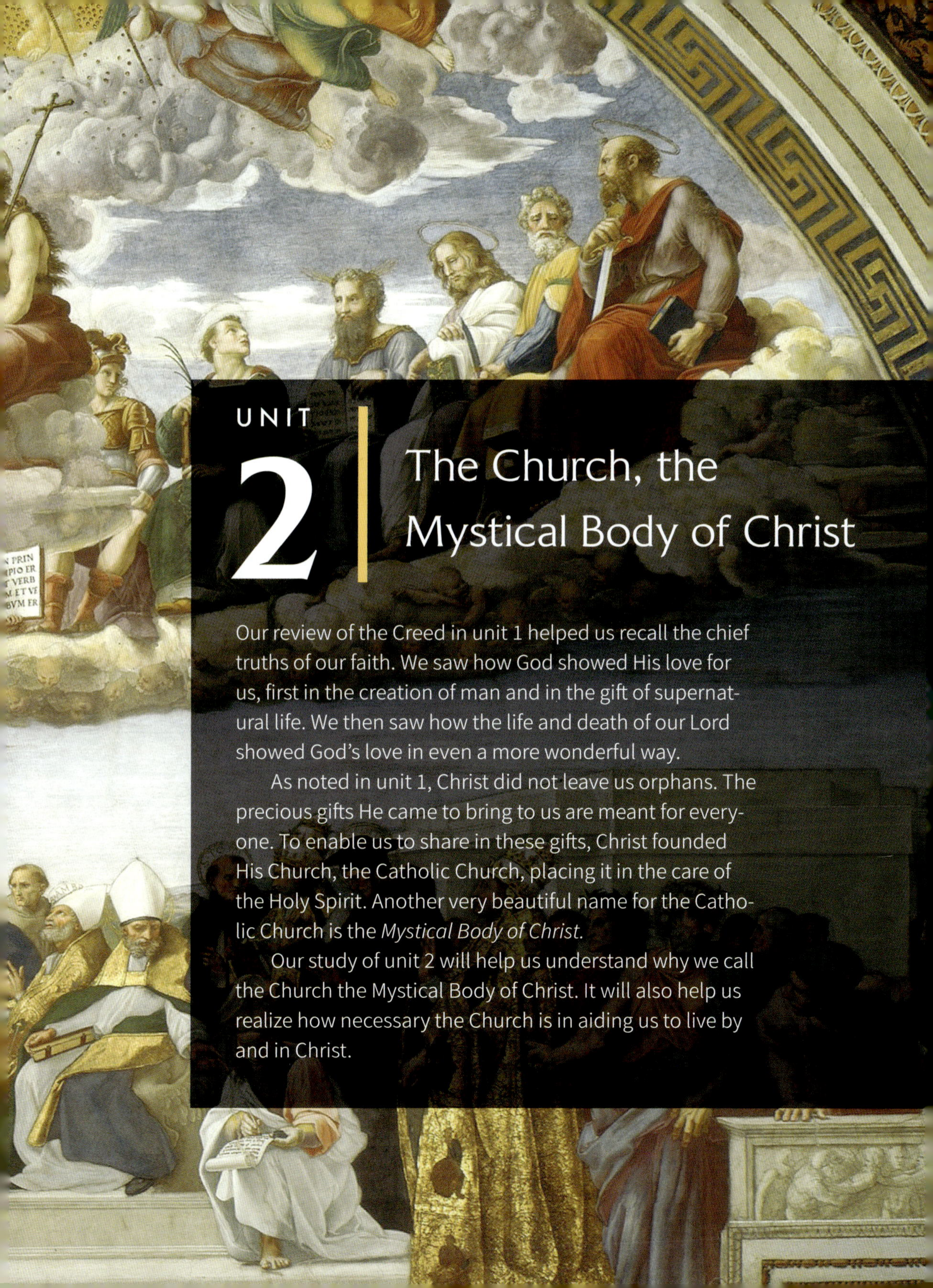

UNIT

2 The Church, the Mystical Body of Christ

Our review of the Creed in unit 1 helped us recall the chief truths of our faith. We saw how God showed His love for us, first in the creation of man and in the gift of supernatural life. We then saw how the life and death of our Lord showed God's love in even a more wonderful way.

As noted in unit 1, Christ did not leave us orphans. The precious gifts He came to bring to us are meant for everyone. To enable us to share in these gifts, Christ founded His Church, the Catholic Church, placing it in the care of the Holy Spirit. Another very beautiful name for the Catholic Church is the *Mystical Body of Christ.*

Our study of unit 2 will help us understand why we call the Church the Mystical Body of Christ. It will also help us realize how necessary the Church is in aiding us to live by and in Christ.

CHAPTER 5

Jesus Christ Founds the Church

Christ came to save us. With the fall of our first parents, sin entered into the world and we lost God's friendship. But "God so loved the world as to give his only-begotten Son" (Jn. 3:16) to regain for us the friendship with God which we had lost.

Through His holy life, bitter Passion, and painful death, Jesus reopened the gates of heaven and merited for all men the graces necessary for salvation. It was possible for Jesus, by Himself, to bestow the merits of His Passion and death on humanity. But He wanted to let us share in His work of redemption. He wished to give every person of every generation the blessings of His Passion and death through His Church. Pius XII has told us that this true Church of Jesus Christ is the Mystical Body of Christ. In this chapter we shall examine what it means when we call the Church the Mystical Body of Christ. To do so, we shall study the Church first as a Body, then as the Body of Christ, and finally as the Mystical Body of Christ.

The Church Is a Body

A body is something that we can see and touch and feel. It is made up of many different parts, and each part is firmly attached to the body. The different parts of the body work together to help the whole.

Watch Jack play ball in the warm sunshine after school. When he dashes to catch the ball, he first looks to see where it will fall.

His strong legs then carry him swiftly to it and his arms stretch out to catch the flying ball. If all parts of his body and mind work well together, Jack will catch the ball.

Our body takes care of its different parts, to keep them alive and well and growing. The food that we eat, for example, must first be digested before it can be of any help to the body. Even then, it must be carried to the various parts of the body by the blood. Each part of the body gets exactly what it needs. In this way our body lives, and keeps well, and grows.

This is the way the human body is made and acts. Christ's Church is in a way like our body. Like our body, the Church is something that can be seen. It is *visible,* that is, can be seen, because its members can be seen and it has a visible head, the pope, who takes the place of its *invisible* head, Jesus Christ. Paul wrote to his converts in the city of Colossae: "[Christ] is the head of his body, the Church" (Col. 1:18). The Church also is made up of a number of parts, united to form *one* whole. As Paul says: "For as the body is one and has many members, and all the members of the body, many as they are, form one body, so also is it with Christ" (1 Cor. 12:12). The members of our body do not all have the same part to play, but all are needed for its well-being. The legs do not see, the eyes do not hear. Without them, however, we could not run and see. The same is true of Christ's Body, the Church. The men and women who are its members do not all have the same duties and vocations, yet all are necessary for its well-being and all together are united in Christ. St. Paul teaches this truth in his letter to the Christians at Rome (Rom. 12:4–5).

> *"About Jesus Christ and the Church, I simply know they're just one thing, and we shouldn't complicate the matter."*
>
> *—St. Joan of Arc*

A human body grows and develops. It requires food to live, and the services of a doctor if we become ill or are injured. Here too Christ's Body, the Church, is much like our body. And Christ, its all-wise and all-loving Founder, has instituted seven channels of life-giving grace, the sacraments, to bestow His life on us, the members of His body. Baptism brings the supernatural life of grace to us, the members of His Body. Confirmation strengthens this life. It gives Christ's members power to live like Christ, and to fight, with Him, against the forces of evil. The Holy Eucharist brings the living Christ into each of His members, and nourishes the Christ-life in them. Penance and Reconciliation heals those members who have suffered wounds or have become injured along the way. It even brings back the life of grace to those who may have lost it through their sins. Matrimony joins a Christian man and woman in marriage. It unites their love with the love of Christ. It gives them the grace to raise children who will be worthy members of the Mystical Body. Holy Orders gives priests the power to pass on the Christ-life to the members of the Mystical Body. Finally, Anointing of the Sick prepares the members of Christ's Body for death, and for their face-to-face meeting with Christ, their Head.

The Church Is the Body of Jesus Christ

The Church is the Body of Jesus Christ because Christ is the Founder and Head of this Body and is present in all of us, His members.

While Jesus was living on earth, He picked twelve Apostles. Most of them were poor fishermen from Galilee. Jesus was going to make them "fishers of men" (Mt. 4:19). He picked one of the twelve, Simon Peter, and made him the chief Apostle. It was Peter to whom our Lord said: ". . . thou art Peter [the Rock], and upon this rock I will build my Church, and the gates of hell shall not prevail against it" (Mt. 16:18). To Peter, Christ gave the keys to His kingdom and the power to bind and to loose, that is, to command and pardon. For Peter, Christ offered special prayers to His heavenly Father that his faith might be strong. Christ also prayed that he might "strengthen" his fellow apostles and the new members of Christ's body (Lk. 22:32). The powers given to Peter, and to the popes after him, are not theirs; they are Christ's. He alone is the Head of His Body, the Church. Peter and the popes act in place of Him. Christ is the true Head, the true Vine. To share His life we must "abide" in Him. As He told us, "I am the vine, you are the branches. He who abides in me, and I in him, he bears much fruit; for without me you can do nothing" (Jn. 15:5).

When Christ died on the cross and rose from the dead, He showed that He is God. He draws all men to Himself (Jn. 12:32). By His death on the cross, Jesus opened up fountains of grace for His Body, the Church, to help it to teach, to rule, and to make its members holy. As head of the Church, Christ is the supreme "shepherd and guardian of [our] souls" (1 Pet. 2:25).

When Christ was hanging from the cross, a soldier's lance pierced His side. Pope Pius XII tells us that the Church, Christ's Mystical Body, was born then. Later, after His ascension, our Lord sent the Holy Spirit to His Church, to remain with it for all times, and to unite its members in love and faith.

Do you remember how the Holy Spirit came down upon the Apostles?

It was fifty days after the Resurrection, ten days after the Ascension. The Apostles were gathered in a large room. Suddenly there was a great noise from Heaven. It sounded like a mighty wind and filled the entire house. Then the Apostles saw tongues of fire, which settled on their heads. The Apostles were filled with the Holy Spirit. In this way the Apostles received the power of the Holy Spirit. Try to understand what we mean when we speak of the Church.

The Church is Christ adoring God the Father and we adore with and in Him.

The Church is Christ thanking God the Father for His blessings and we thank God through and with Christ.

The Church is Christ asking God for His blessings and we ask with and in Him.

The Church is Christ making up to God for the sins committed and we make up with and in Him.

The Church is Christ at prayer in all of us when we pray.

The Church is Christ bringing divine life to us through the sacraments, and making us like Christ.

The Church is Christ helping us gain grace through the sacramentals.

The Church is Christ re-living His life in His members through the liturgical year.

The Church is Christ the King, teaching and ruling us, His members; it is Christ the Priest redeeming us from sin and making us holy with His divine life.

The Church Is the Mystical Body of Christ

We have now learned why the Church is called a Body and why it is called the Body of Christ. It is a *Body* because it can be seen and is made up of a number of parts. It is the Body *of Christ* because He is its Founder and true Head, who gives life to us, its members.

Why is the Church called a "Mystical" Body? The word *mystical* is used to show us that the Church is different from other bodies. It is supernatural: The Holy Spirit is the soul of the Mystical Body.

Our body has parts, such as hands and feet. We do not see hands and feet living by themselves. These parts belong to the whole body. Christ's Mystical Body also has a number of parts or members. These members are men and women, boys and girls. They belong to the whole body which we call the Body of Christ. That is why we can say that the Mystical Body is in some way like our own.

The men and women who are members of Christ's Body still have their own individual selves. They are not only parts of Christ's Body. They are also bodies themselves. That is why there is a difference between the Church or Christ's Body and our own. But the bodies of Christians also live by the supernatural life which the Holy Spirit gives them as members of the Mystical Body.

Sometimes the students of a school are conceived of as a "body", that is, the "student body." How is a body like this different from the Mystical Body of Christ? You and your classmates are joined together to learn. The members of Christ's Church are joined together to gain heaven. But, in addition, the Holy Spirit lives in the Mystical Body. He unites the members of that Body by giving them the gifts of faith, hope, and charity. These bonds are much stronger than those which unite the members of a "student body."

Since Christ the Head sends His own spirit into the Church and into all its members, the members of the Church are joined with Christ to make a new body. It is the Holy Spirit who makes and keeps the Mystical Body of Christ one and united. This new body, His Mystical Body, has a

Head which is Christ;
Soul which is the Holy Spirit; and
Members. We are the members.

FOR ME TO REVIEW

Catechism Lesson

115. Q. What is the Church?

A. The Church is the congregation of all those who profess the faith of Christ, partake of the same sacraments, and are governed by their lawful pastors under one visible Head.

117. Q. Who is the visible Head of the Church?

A. Our Holy Father the pope, the bishop of Rome, is the Vicar of Christ on earth and the visible Head of the Church.

118. Q. Why is the pope, the bishop of Rome, the visible Head of the Church?

A. The pope, the bishop of Rome, is the visible Head of the Church because he is the successor of St. Peter, whom Christ made the chief of the Apostles and the visible Head of the Church.

119. Q. Who are the successors of the other Apostles?
A. The successors of the other Apostles are the bishops of the Holy Catholic Church.

996. Q. How should Christians look upon the priests of the Church?
A. Christians should look upon the priests of the Church as the messengers of God and the dispensers of His mysteries.

997. Q. How do we know that the priests of the Church are the messengers of God?
A. We know that the priests of the Church are the messengers of God, because Christ said to His Apostles, and through them to their successors: "As the Father hath sent Me, I also send you"; that is to say, to preach the true religion, to administer the sacraments, to offer Sacrifice, and to do all manner of good for the salvation of souls.

116. Q. Who is the invisible Head of the Church?
A. Jesus Christ is the invisible Head of the Church.

Questions

1. What is the Church?
2. Who founded the Church?
3. Who was the first pope?
4. To whom did Christ give the power to teach, to sanctify, and to rule His members?
5. Why do we call the Church the Mystical Body of Christ?
6. Explain: "The Church is Christ in the world today."
7. How does the Church differ from an ordinary club or society, like the "student body" in your school?

FOR ME TO REMEMBER

1. Jesus founded the Church.
2. Jesus Christ is the *invisible* Head of the Church.
3. St. Peter was the first pope. He was the first *visible* head of the Church.
4. *Visible* means that it can be seen.
5. Christ gave the Apostles and their successors the power to teach, to sanctify, and to rule the members of the Church.
6. The Church is called the Body of Christ because Jesus is its Head and Ruler and we are its members.

FOR ME TO DO

1. Tell in your own words the story of the founding of the Catholic Church. Draw pictures of as many facts as you can.
2. Dramatize the scene in which Christ makes St. Peter the head of the Church.
3. Discuss ways you can show that Jesus Christ is the invisible Head of the Church.
4. Illustrate the life of the present Holy Father, the pope. Explain why he is the successor of St. Peter.

CHAPTER 6

The Members of the Mystical Body of Christ

Do you know that even before God created us He thought about each one of us and loved us? He wanted us, with millions of other boys and girls, men and women, to belong to His great family on earth. He wanted us to belong to His Church, the Mystical Body of Christ.

The members of the Mystical Body of Christ are all those who are baptized and who profess the true faith. We must count as members of the Mystical Body not only those who are very holy, but sinful members also. Our Lord, full of pity for sinners, lets them continue to be parts of His Mystical Body. These sinful members may even have committed mortal sin; while in that condition they can never get to heaven, yet they belong to Christ's Body as long as they profess the Catholic religion.

We should hate sin because it weakens the members of Christ's Body. But, although we should hate sin, we must not hate the people who commit sin. If we are good members of Christ's Body we should love one another. A member who is weak because of sin can be made strong in the Church. Can you say how?

Members Are Joined With Christ and With One Another

Just before Jesus left the room where He ate the Last Supper with His Apostles, He spoke to them to encourage and to comfort them. Jesus knew that they were sad because He was going to leave them. But Jesus told them that although He would no longer walk and talk with them, He would always be very close to them.

It was hard for the Apostles to understand what Jesus was trying to tell them. So, to help them understand what He meant, Jesus told them a parable in which He compared Himself to a vine. A *parable* is a short story used to teach something. Jesus said: "I am the vine, you are the branches. He who abides in me, and I in him, bears much fruit; for without me you can do nothing" (Jn. 15:5).

Now, the Apostles knew what a vine was because they had seen many of them growing. They also knew that branches get their life from the vine. Slowly they began to see what Jesus meant when He said that He would always be with them. Jesus meant that He and the Apostles would always be very closely united. The Apostles also came to understand that they could receive the divine life of grace only when they were united to Jesus. "For without me you can do nothing."

To understand just how closely we are joined with Christ in the Church, let us think about the words Jesus Christ spoke to the Apostles. Christ told the Apostles that He is the living Vine and we are the branches of that living Vine. If a branch is not joined to the living Vine, no fruit can grow on it. In the same way, if we are not joined to Christ we do not have Christ's divine life in us. We can then do nothing to save ourselves or others.

In the Church the members are very closely joined because God the Holy Spirit is in them. It is He who helps them gain eternal life. He is always with them. He helps them to do their duty. The more holy they become the more help they will get. In this way Christ is always making the Church grow more and more holy.

In the Church the members are also closely joined with one another and with God by the virtues of faith, hope, and charity.

We are joined by *faith* because we believe in God and the truths He has revealed. We all want to be with God in heaven and trust in Him as the giver of everlasting happiness. We are thus joined with one another by *hope.* But it is *charity* or love, more than faith and hope, that keeps us close to Christ. If we love Christ, He will come into our hearts and love us too. But we cannot love Christ without loving all those for whom He died on the cross. "If you love me, keep my commandments" (Jn. 14:15).

"By this will all men know that you are my disciples, if you have love for one another" (Jn. 13:35). These are the words Christ, the Head, speaks to all His members. The more we love one another and help one another, the more closely shall we be united to Christ. Also, the more we love Christ, the more closely shall we be united with one another in love.

Our Duties as Members of the Mystical Body of Christ

What a glorious and blessed thing it is to be a member of the Catholic Church! In the Catholic Church we are members of one Body. We are led by one Head, Jesus Christ. We are united and filled with grace by the Holy Spirit. We are taught to believe one faith. While on this earth we are fed with the Holy Eucharist and look forward to everlasting happiness in heaven.

Do you ever think of the goodness and generosity of Jesus Christ? Do you ever wonder how best you can show your love and appreciation for being a member of the Mystical Body of Christ? Here is how.

Adore and worship God through Christ by taking part in the various liturgies of the Church. Give thanks to Christ for calling us to take part in His divine life. Honor and obey the Church because Christ gave it the authority to rule over us. Love the sacraments which give divine life to our souls. Love all the things the Church does when it honors God in the name of its members.

Our love for the Church should include all its members because Christ is in the Church and in each member. We must love especially those who are weak, those who are sick, and those who are poor. God loves these members in a special way. Whatever we do to help them, He considers it as being done to Himself. Remember His words: "whoever gives you a cup of water to drink in my name, because you are Christ's, amen I say to you, he shall not lose his reward" (Mk. 9:40).

But we must not think it enough to love only those who are joined with us in the Church. Christ loves all men. We must follow His example. We must also love those who are not Catholic, or Christian. For Christ also died for them, and they are made by God. We must help them find Christ.

At the Last Supper, Christ prayed for all people, "for those also who through their word are to believe in me, that all may be one, even as you, Father, in me and I in you; that they also may be one in us, that the world may believe that you have sent me" (Jn. 17:20–21).

We show our love for the Church by working hard at all times to help the Church grow. We help the Church grow especially when we live as good Catholics and give good example.

We can also help the Church grow by our prayers. Pray every day for all the members of the Mystical Body of Christ. Pray especially for the Holy Father, for the bishops, priests, sisters, and brothers who have been called by God to do His work. Pray for parents, that they may raise their children as worthy members of Christ's Body. Pray for all men, that they may all be one in love and that all may belong to the true Vine, Jesus Christ. Pray especially for those who are not yet members of the Catholic Church.

What greater proof of love for the Church can we show than by imitating Christ in making sacrifices! Christ gladly suffered pain and sorrow for the love of His Church when He was dying on the cross. Christ also left a share of suffering for each of us. If we join our sufferings with the sufferings of Christ, we shall someday be with Christ in heaven.

FOR ME TO REVIEW

Catechism Lesson

107. Q. What is faith?

A. Faith is a theological virtue by which we firmly believe the truths which God has revealed.

108. Q. What is hope?

A. Hope is a theological virtue by which we firmly trust that God will give us eternal life and the means to obtain it.

109. Q. What is charity?

A. Charity is a theological virtue by which we love God above all things for His own sake, and our neighbor as ourselves for the love of God.

120. Q. Why did Christ found the Church?

A. Christ founded the Church to teach, govern, sanctify, and save all men.

Questions

1. Who belongs to the Mystical Body of Christ?
2. What is faith?
3. What is hope?
4. What is charity?
5. How are we joined to one another by faith, hope, and charity?
6. Make a list of duties of the members of the Mystical Body.

FOR ME TO REMEMBER

1. Members of the Mystical Body of Christ are baptized persons who profess the true faith.
2. A *parable* is a story used by our Lord to teach a lesson.
3. Members of the Mystical Body are joined with Christ and with one another by baptism and by faith.
4. Our charity should include all members of the Church, and indeed *all* men, for all men are called to be members of the Church.
5. We are obliged to help the Church grow. We can do this by prayer, a holy life and sacrifice.

FOR ME TO DO

1. Draw a vine. Underneath it write the verse, "I am the Vine, you are the branches." Explain the meaning of this quotation.
2. Find stories illustrating various means of helping the growth of the Catholic Church.
3. Learn the *Corporal Works of Mercy.* Bring in pictures or make drawings illustrating each.
4. Learn about opportunities for mission work in your home parish.
5. Review the Acts of Faith, Hope, and Charity.
6. Make up a prayer in which you will ask God to give many boys and girls a call to His service.

Summary of Unit 2

Christ founded the Catholic Church in order to continue His priestly work in the world for all time. The Catholic Church is the Mystical Body of Christ because Christ is its Head and Ruler.

Jesus Christ gave His Apostles the power to teach, to make holy, and to rule the faithful on earth. He gave special authority to St. Peter by making him the head of the Apostles.

Today the bishops, like the Apostles, have the power to teach, to sanctify, and to rule the Church. The priests share these powers.

The members of the Mystical Body of Christ are all those who are baptized and who profess the true faith. They are closely joined with one another and with Christ by faith, hope, and charity. Charity includes all people, even those who are not of our faith. It is our sacred duty to help them find Christ.

Write your answers on a separate sheet of paper

Part 1 Yes or No

Read each question carefully. Then answer yes or no.

1. Did the Holy Spirit come down on the Apostles forty days after Easter?
2. Is the Church made up of those who are baptized, united in the same true faith, and obedient to the pope?
3. Is your non-Catholic friend called to be a member of the Mystical Body of Christ?
4. Are the Acts of Faith, Hope, and Charity ways of worshiping God?
5. Is the pope the true visible head of the Church?
6. Is the Holy Spirit the soul of the Church?
7. If you invite a non-Catholic friend to Mass are you acting like a good member of the Church?
8. Do we help spread the Faith when we live a good Catholic life?
9. Do only those who are in the state of grace belong to the Mystical Body of Christ?
10. When Jesus said, "I am the Vine, and you are the branches," did He mean that we are members of His Mystical Body?

Part 2 Completion

Complete each statement. Use the words below to help you.

charity	St. Peter	bishops
Pentecost	pope	parable
Church	Mystical Body	
Jesus Christ	Apostles	

1. The Apostle who was made head of the Church was. . . . . . .
2. The birthday of the Catholic Church is. . . . . . .
3. The Head of the Mystical Body is. . . . . . .
4. When we give offerings for the missions we practice the virtue of. . . . . . .
5. The successors of the Apostles are. . . . . . .
6. Christ first gave the. . . . . . the power to teach, sanctify, and rule the members of His. . . . . . .
7. A story which contains a hidden truth is a. . . . . . .
8. The union of all members of the Church with Christ the Head is the. . . . . . .
9. The founder of the Catholic Church is. . . . . . .
10. The visible head of the Church is the. . . . . . .

UNIT 3 The Sacred Liturgy and the Church Year: Living What We Believe

Imagine living at the time when our Lord went about doing good, working miracles, teaching, and showing people the way to heaven, to God. Imagine being present on Calvary when Christ was dying for you. Would you not desire to prove your love for Him by being true and loyal to the end? It is beautiful and wonderful to think of such things. For faithful Catholics, these meditations become a reality. Did you know that in the Holy Sacrifice of the Mass we receive the opportunity to be with Christ on Calvary? What an incredible grace! Today we have the joy of belonging to Christ's Mystical Body, the Church, of which Christ is the Head and we are the members. Christ lived long ago. He lives once again in the members of His Mystical Body to continue, through the liturgy, the work of giving glory to His Father, of making men holy, and of uniting them to Himself on earth and in heaven.

Every year Christ in His Church re-lives His life so that He may share it with us. Each year Christ's life is made present to us. This is called the Liturgical Year or the Church Year. It is by living the Liturgical Year that we live Christ's life with Him.

By living with the Church with Christ, we can continually receive an increase of His life, the life of grace. We can "grow up" in Christ. We hope to show you how in unit 3. These are very old traditions and inexhaustible mysteries. You will come back to the things you learn this year in the years to come.

CHAPTER 7

The Liturgy as Christ Continuing His Priestly Work

In unit 2 we learned that the Church which Jesus founded is called the *Mystical Body of Christ.* We know that we became members of this great body at Baptism. We also learned that, in His Church, Christ has closely united us to Himself and to one another. Let us now try to understand how Christ lives and acts in His Mystical Body, the Church.

Christ came to earth to give glory to His Father and to make men holy. The people who were blessed to see our Lord and talk with Him were not the only ones whom Christ came to save. Christ came to save all men.

Christ lives and acts in the liturgy of the Church, that is, He lives and acts in the Holy Sacrifice of the Mass, the Divine Office, the sacraments, the sacramentals, and the Liturgical Year.

The Meaning of Liturgy

The exterior and interior worship by which we honor, glorify, and adore God is called the *Sacred Liturgy.*

You have often heard the story of the birth of Christ. Can you tell the story of how the shepherds came from the hillsides to honor the child of whom they had heard wonderful things?

When we assist at Holy Mass, we show by our actions that we adore God. Here we are performing an action like that of the shepherds who knelt down before the Christ Child. Our actions at Mass are an example of *exterior worship.* It is the official worship

of the Church in which we take an active part. But it is more important that we worship God with our hearts and minds, that we give ourselves wholly to Christ so that we live through Him, with Him, and in Him and in this way give glory to the heavenly Father. This is *interior worship.*

What Is the Sacred Liturgy?

The word *liturgy* means *worship,* especially the *public worship* offered to God. Christ is the head of the Church, therefore, we can say that the Sacred Liturgy is Christ the God Man, as our high priest and as head of the human race, praying to God the Father. The liturgy is Christ's act of perfect praise and adoration to God the Father. The liturgy is the prayer of deepest thanksgiving which Christ offers to God for the greatness and goodness of God in Himself and for the gifts He has given men. The liturgy is Christ, God the Son and our brother, pouring forth infinitely powerful prayers in atonement for our sins. The liturgy is Christ begging God to give us the gifts and graces need for our salvation.

Because we are truly members of Christ's Body, we participate in this liturgy. In the liturgy we join Christ in these prayers of adoration, of thanksgiving, of satisfaction and of petition, in the Mass. But the liturgy is also Christ making the world holy by the

teaching of His Church, especially by uniting us in His Body with Himself by means of the sacraments.

The liturgy is the work of Christ in giving us that wonderful new and higher life which we call supernatural life, a life which is a sharing in the life and graces of God Himself by Baptism, Confirmation, and the Holy Eucharist—uniting us with Him on the cross in the sacrifice of the Holy Eucharist and feeding us with His Body and Blood, filling us with divine strength and holiness in Holy Communion.

The liturgy is Christ in the confessional raising His hand to absolve us through the priest. The liturgy sees Christ at the side of the sick and the dying, giving them the strength of the last anointing in Anointing of the Sick.

The liturgy is Christ praying and teaching us to pray as He did when He taught the Our Father and when He prayed in Gethsemani.

The liturgy is Christ our great High Priest offering Himself crucified on the cross to God the Father in that infinitely powerful sacrifice of love and obedience which turns away God's anger and makes us "children of God."

The liturgy is Christ in His Church blessing a man and a woman with special graces when they unite themselves for His purposes in the holy sacrament of Matrimony.

Words of Our Lord

> *"I pray for them; not for the world do I pray, but for those whom thou hast given me, because they are thine; and all things that are mine are thine, and thine are mine; and I am glorified in them. And I am no longer in the world, but these are in the world, and I am coming to thee. Holy Father, keep in thy name those whom thou hast given me, that they may be one even as we are" (John 17:9–11).*

The liturgy is Christ taking those who offer themselves to Him completely and making them into saints, that is, into other Christs. Then their every thought and act is according to the desires of the Sacred Heart of Jesus; then men see and feel the great virtues Christ practiced and preached: faith, and hope, and especially love; prudence, justice, fortitude, and temperance; obedience, courage, humility, and purity. The liturgy is God in this world trying to help men become like God.

Study the chart on the following pages. Perhaps it will help you to understand more clearly how the Church in her liturgy continues the work of Jesus Christ on earth.

JESUS CHRIST		
	In His Public Life	**In the Liturgy**
TEACHES	Sermon on the Mount. Christ taught the people how they must live as members of His Church. He also told them about the reward awaiting those who would follow His teachings.	Christ continues to teach us what He wants us to know about Himself and heaven in the readings during Mass.
SANCTIFIES	"I came that they may have life, and have it more abundantly" (Jn. 10:10). By these words Christ promised to make men sharers in His divine life.	Christ present in the sacraments brings us His grace, makes us sharers in His life, and saves our souls.
OFFERS SACRIFICE	At the Last Supper Jesus changed bread and wine into His Body and Blood to be our food and drink. On Calvary Jesus gave Himself to God the Father for our sins. On Calvary Jesus gave His life as our Gift to God.	Holy Sacrifice of the Mass. The priests have the power, invested in them by Christ, to change bread and wine into the Body and Blood of Jesus Christ. In the Mass Christ acts through the priest and offers His own Body and Blood to the heavenly Father.
PRAYS	When Christ was on earth He prayed always; sometimes He spent whole nights in prayer. In the Garden, Christ prayed that the cup of suffering might, if possible, pass away, but immediately followed with an act of resignation to the will of His Father. On the cross Christ begged for pardon for those who were putting Him to death.	The Church prays continually to God, especially during the Mass. With Jesus we adore God, we thank Him, we ask for favors, and we beg His pardon for our many sins. Almost every prayer of the Church ends with the words: "Through Our Lord Jesus Christ" to show that it is through Christ that we go to God.
		The Church worships God by her official prayer, which is the Divine Office.

Christ Acts in the Liturgy

Christ is present in every religious action of the Church. What Christ did when He was on earth He continues today in the liturgy. In the holy sacrifice of the Mass, our Savior continues the sacrifice of the cross. As our great High Priest He constantly offers a sacrifice of praise and adoration to His heavenly Father. At the same time, He offers Himself as the perfect Victim for the sins of men. Christ is, therefore, the One who offers and at the same time the One who is offered. He is both priest and victim.

At every Mass the priest, acting in Christ's name and on our behalf, offers Jesus Christ to God the Father. Every time we assist at the Holy Sacrifice of the Mass we join our prayers with those of Christ and the priest and we pray with Him.

When Jesus Christ offers Himself to the heavenly Father through the priest, He also offers us, the members of His Mystical Body, to God through Himself. Of course we must be willing to offer ourselves to God, or Christ cannot offer us together with Himself.

To give or to increase the life of grace in our souls, Christ acts through the sacraments. When the priest or deacon baptizes, Christ washes the soul of original sin and makes it live. In every confession, it is Christ who forgives. Each day He offers Himself as our true food in the Holy Eucharist. He comes into our hearts to make us live with His own life. The sick and dying are helped by Him in Anointing of the Sick. He gives many graces to the bride and groom at every Catholic wedding and continues to bless them throughout their married life. In Confirmation, He strengthens us to be soldiers of Christ. In Holy Orders, He pours out the power of His own divine priesthood upon a young man whom He has chosen to carry on His priestly work.

Through the sacramentals of the Church, Christ blesses His people in all their needs, and helps them to receive more grace.

In the daily prayer of the Church, the Divine Office, Christ is praying through His Mystical Body. With each liturgical season, Christ's life is made present again from His birth to His sufferings and death.

Thus we see that Christ is truly present in the liturgy of the Church. In the liturgy He continues to carry on His work of praising the Father and giving eternal life to men.

Our Part in the Liturgy

We must take part in the liturgy of the Church with our whole minds and hearts if we wish to have union with Christ. The closer we are to Christ, the greater is our share in His divine life. We come to desire what He desires and love what He loves. This will be easier to understand if you remember the time you played with a magnet and a piece of steel. What happened when you placed the piece of steel close to the ends of the magnet? The magnet, without losing any of its pulling force, put some of its power into the steel. In fact, the steel, as long as it clung to the magnet, could even pick up another piece of steel.

> *"I . . . will draw all things to myself" (Jn 12:32).*

Our Lord is like that magnet. Through the liturgy of the Church He draws us to Himself. Not only that, but He shares His divine life with us. Then, once we are closely united to Him, He uses us as His instruments in lifting others up to His divine love. "And I, if I be lifted up from the earth, will draw all things to myself" (Jn. 12:32). When we look at our Lord on the cross, how true these words ring!

The Books of the Church

The Church uses several books to carry out its liturgical worship. The most important are the missal, and the breviary.

The *missal* contains all the prayers recited or sung at Mass. The missal also contains the most important actions the priest and people perform during the celebration of the Holy Sacrifice of the Mass. Some of the prayers remain the same in each Mass, while others change from day to day and during the different liturgical seasons of the Church Year. The missal is used by the priest at the altar and by many of the faithful assisting at Mass. This book can help us take an active part in the public worship of the Church.

The *breviary* is the prayer book used by priests, consecrated men and women, and many lay people who recite the Divine Office. The Church requires the Divine Office to be read or sung by priests and members of certain consecrated and religious orders. The breviary corresponds with the Mass of the day and the different liturgical seasons. It provides a daily rhythm to the members of the Church so that the entire Body of Christ lives and breathes according to the same mind and spirit.

FOR ME TO REVIEW

Questions

1. What is the liturgy? Give two or three definitions and illustrate each.
2. What is the difference between *exterior* and *interior* worship? Which is more important? Explain your answer.
3. Why does the Church insist that we pray? Give examples of Christ at prayer.

4. Christ is present in every liturgical action. Prove this statement by using examples taken from this unit.
5. How can we become more and more like Jesus Christ?
6. Give the names of the chief books of the Church. In one or two sentences explain each.

FOR ME TO REMEMBER

1. Jesus Christ came to earth to glorify His Father and to sanctify man.
2. Jesus lives His life on earth again in the sacred liturgy.
3. Public worship is exterior worship.
4. When we worship God with our hearts and minds, we practice *interior worship.*
5. The *sacred liturgy* is exterior and interior worship by which the Mystical Body of Christ honors, glorifies, and adores God.
6. Christ acts in every liturgical action of the Church.
7. Through the sacraments Christ gives or increases divine life in us.
8. The closer we are united with Christ, the greater is our share in His divine life.
9. The most important books used by the Church are: the missal and the breviary.

FOR ME TO DO

1. Give the meaning of each of the following words as used in this chapter. Also use each word in a sentence.

liturgy	interior	exterior
worship	supernatural	incorporating

2. Collect or draw pictures illustrating the various meanings of liturgy.
3. Read the Sermon on the Mount. Briefly tell what each of the beatitudes means.
4. Discuss with the class ways in which you can participate in the liturgy.
5. George heard a friend of his say that *Jesus is like a magnet.* Explain to him what is meant by this expression.

CHAPTER 8
The Mass, the Crowning Act of the Liturgy

The Holy Sacrifice of the Mass is the heart of the liturgical life of the Church. It is the high point and center of the Catholic faith. It is the most holy and sublime prayer in the world. In it we adore and glorify the heavenly Father in the most perfect way. It is the renewal of Calvary in which Christ daily offers Himself to the Father. Because we are members of Christ's Body, we too can offer ourselves together with Jesus as our Gift to God in the sacrifice of the Mass. Every time the Mass is offered "the merits won by the Divine Redeemer upon the Cross are distributed to the faithful."

The Meaning of the Word Sacrifice

In the Mass the sacrifice of the cross takes place again. *The Mass is the Sacrifice of the New Law in which Jesus Christ, through the priest, offers Himself to God in an unbloody manner under the appearance of bread and wine.*

Since the Mass is a sacrifice, it is important to know the meaning of the word *sacrifice.* We often say that a mother is sacrificing herself for her children. What does that mean? The mother is giving up sleep, alone time, rest, fine clothes and food, in order that her children might have what they need. Soldiers make great sacrifices when they join the army. Can you tell why? Sometimes a little boy is sorry for the extra expense that he caused

by throwing a baseball through a window. Instead of asking his parents for the money, he offers to go without the new baseball mitt that Dad promised him. This is the little boy's sacrifice.

Whenever we suffer, whenever we go through something painful for others in order to show our love for them, we are making a sacrifice. Whenever we give up something that we love very much for another person in order to make him happy and prove our love for him, we are making a sacrifice. A sacrifice is like a gift.

There is, however, another more important meaning of sacrifice, and this is the one we have in mind when we say the Mass is a sacrifice.

> *"It would be easier for the world to survive without the sun than to do so without the Holy Mass."*
>
> —*St. Pio of Pietrelcina*

Sacrifices of the Old Law

God is holy, infinitely great, and all powerful. Men and all things depend entirely on Him. From earliest times men have understood this. They have known that they are obliged to worship God and to offer to Him in adoration the very best things they have—even their own lives. But God has forbidden men to take their physical lives. Therefore, men took something they owned which was very valuable and offered it to God as a substitute for themselves. Then they destroyed it in His honor, to make up for their past sins. They offered sacrifices of their finest lambs, goats, and calves, killing them and laying them on the altar. They offered sacrifices of their grain and fruit, bread and wine.

In the Old Testament, the Israelites gave gifts of fruits and animals to God. They burned their gifts to prove to God that every bit was for Him and that they did not want to keep any part.

The sacrifices of the Old Testament were pleasing to God but they were not perfect. The persons offering them and the things they offered were mere creatures, therefore they could not honor God enough and redeem men from sin. Only God Himself could do this.

The Sacrifice of Calvary

Because of His great love for us, our Lord gave us the perfect sacrifice. He knew better than anyone else how to honor God, how to thank Him and how to bring us the forgiveness that we need. He would offer His life to God for us. He would be the Victim for us. He Himself would be the true and perfect gift.

He did what He would not allow us to do: He offered Himself as the victim for the sacrifice. At the Last Supper, He offered Himself in an unbloody manner to God. On Good Friday, Jesus made His offering in a bloody manner to God the Father on the altar of the cross. He, the High Priest, willingly offered Himself to His heavenly Father so that we could have life and have it fully. Now He offers Himself daily on the altar during Mass, where He applies to us the merits of His death on the cross, and offers Himself in the same unbloody manner as He offered Himself at the Last Supper.

How can we ever thank Jesus enough for making up to His Father for everything we owe Him!

"The Holy Sacrifice, because it makes present the one sacrifice of Christ the Savior and includes the Church's offering. The terms holy sacrifice of the Mass, 'sacrifice of praise,' spiritual sacrifice, pure and holy sacrifice are also used, since it completes and surpasses all the sacrifices of the Old Covenant."

—Catechism of the Catholic Church, 1330

The Mass, the Central and Supreme Act

Our Lord's whole life—everything He said and did—led up to Calvary, where He gave up His life for the salvation of man. In the same way the Holy Sacrifice of the Mass is the most wonderful gift, the center, the heart of the liturgical life of the Church. It is the worship Christ offers to His Father through the members of His Church. On the cross Jesus Christ, the Son of God, won graces for us all and made up for our sins. On our altars the same Christ, acting through His priests, offers His Body and Blood to the Father for us.

The power which the priest has to act in Jesus' name was given on Holy Thursday. During the Last Supper Jesus took bread and wine and changed it into His Body and Blood. He said: "This is my body, which is being given for you; do this in remembrance of me." He then continued: "This cup is the new covenant in my blood, which shall be shed for you" (Lk. 22:19–20). It is really Jesus who offers His sufferings and death for us again.

Purposes of the Sacrifice of the Mass

Do you recall why the people from the earliest days offered sacrifices to God? They wanted to honor and adore their Creator from whom they had received all good things, even life itself.

In the Holy Sacrifice of the Mass we honor and adore God in the way that pleases Him best. This Sacrifice is the public worship which Christ Himself offers, through the members of His Body, to God the Father.

There are four reasons or purposes for which the Holy Sacrifice is offered to God:

1. We belong to God because He is the Creator of heaven and earth and of all things. He is our Lord and Master. We owe Him honor and adoration.

In Holy Mass we offer Jesus Christ as our Gift to God. We do this to show God that we honor and adore Him.

2. Everything that we have—the good things of our earthly life and all spiritual favors—come from God. We owe Him everlasting thanks for His goodness and generosity.

The Holy Sacrifice of the Mass is offered to thank our heavenly Father for His rich blessings and for His many gifts.

3. Every human being has some special needs, either temporal or spiritual. Holy Mother the Church also has needs.

The Mass is offered to beg God for all the favors and blessings which we and the Church always need.

4. Man has been guilty of many sins against God. Jesus became man in order to suffer and die and in this way to make up to God for our sins.

The Mass is offered to the heavenly Father to make up for the sins we have committed and to make amends for them.

In short we can say that the Mass is offered:

1. to adore God,
2. to thank Him for favors received,
3. to ask for new graces,
4. and to satisfy for our sins.

The next time you attend Mass think of these four reasons why Mass is offered. Unite yourself with the priest and make acts of adoration, thanksgiving, petition, and satisfaction.

Three Things Needed for a Sacrifice: Priest, Victim, Altar

Like the sacrifices of the Old Law, the Mass needs three basic things:

(1) priest, (2) victim, and (3) altar.

In the Old Law the victim was an animal, wine, or fruits of the earth. In the Mass the priest and victim are the same. It is Jesus Christ, God-Man, the High Priest, who offers Himself through the hands of a human priest as a victim to His heavenly Father.

Our Part in the Mass

It is important for us to remember that the Mass is the center of the sacred liturgy. Taking part in the Mass is the best way for renewing our divine life. Through the priest, who takes Christ's place, we offer the Mass through Christ, with Christ, and in Christ. Do not forget the words of the Mass: "Pray brethren, that my sacrifice and *yours* may be acceptable to God, the almighty Father." We offer an unbloody sacrifice to God the Father.

We participate in Holy Mass because we, as members of the Mystical Body of Christ, share in His priesthood and "victimhood" as far as we offer ourselves to God. We should try to do our share in the offering of the Mass by assisting with reverence and great devotion. The Mass should be our own expression of adoration, thanksgiving, petition, and atonement for sin.

FOR ME TO REVIEW

Catechism Lesson

876. Q. What happened when our Lord said, "This is My Body; this is My Blood"?

A. When our Lord said, "This is My Body," the substance of the bread was changed into the substance of His Body; when He said, "This is My Blood," the substance of the wine was changed into the substance of His Blood.

892. Q. What do the words "Do this in commemoration of Me" mean?

A. The words "Do this in commemoration of Me" mean: Do what I, Christ, am doing at My Last Supper, namely, changing the substance of bread and wine into the substance of My Body and Blood; and do it in remembrance of Me.

893. Q. How do the priests exercise this power of changing bread and wine into the Body and Blood of Christ?

A. The priests exercise this power of changing bread and wine into the Body and Blood of Christ through the words of Consecration in the Mass, which are words of Christ: "This is My Body; this is My Blood."

917. Q. What is the Mass?

A. The Mass is the unbloody Sacrifice of the body and blood of Christ.

920. Q. Is the Mass the same Sacrifice as that of the Cross?

A. The Mass is the same Sacrifice as that of the Cross.

Questions

1. What is a sacrifice?
2. Why do people offer sacrifice?
3. What three things are needed for a sacrifice?
4. What is the difference between a *bloody* and an *unbloody* sacrifice? Give examples of each.
5. What kind of sacrifice did Christ offer on Calvary?
6. What is the Mass?
7. Is the Mass a real sacrifice? Explain.
8. Who said the first Mass? When and where?
9. When did Jesus give priests the power to celebrate Mass?
10. What sacrifice can we offer at Mass?
11. Why do we say that the Mass is the crowning act of the liturgy?

FOR ME TO REMEMBER

1. The Mass is the heart of the sacred liturgy.
2. The Mass is the same sacrifice as the sacrifice of the cross.
3. Christ instituted the sacrament and sacrifice of the Holy Eucharist at the Last Supper.

4. On Holy Thursday Jesus gave the Apostles the power to change bread and wine into His body and blood.
5. By the words, "Do this in commemoration of me" Jesus gave His Apostles and priests the power to change bread and wine into His body and blood.
6. Mass is offered for four purposes: To adore God, to thank Him, to ask for new graces, and to make satisfaction for sins.
7. In every sacrifice three things are needed: a priest, a victim, and an altar.
8. In the Mass Jesus is at the same time priest and victim.
9. The sacrifices of the Old Law were either bloody or unbloody.
10. The Sacrifice of the Mass is an unbloody sacrifice.

FOR ME TO DO

1. God is a spirit. Explain how we can give God a gift.
2. Spend some time adoring God; thank Him for the many gifts He has given you.
3. Find some pictures of the Last Supper, the Crucifixion, and the Mass. Explain in what way they are similar; in what way they are different. Who is the victim in all three?
4. Draw a picture of a sacrifice in the Old Law.
5. Write a short paragraph telling what is meant by sacrifice.

CHAPTER 9
The Divine Office

It has been said that "prayer" is the "breathing of the Mystical Body." Breath is a sign of life. When we stop breathing we die. To breathe, the Church must pray, and the duty to pray belongs to us who are its members.

Even though Jesus was busy teaching and preparing His Apostles for their work, He still found time to spend the night in prayer. We read that Jesus frequently talked with God, His Father. He set the example for us to pray. *Prayer is the lifting up of our minds and hearts to God.*

Jesus began His work with prayer. To be like Him, we should begin our day by offering it to God through prayer. We know that before Jesus chose His Apostles, before He instituted the Holy Eucharist, and before His Passion and death, He prayed to His heavenly Father to give Him strength to do His will. His last hours were one long prayer. He prayed first for His Apostles, then for all men; then He prayed for Himself so that He would have strength in His agony in the garden.

Christ prays in the world today as He did while He was on earth. He prays now through the members of His Mystical Body, especially in its official daily prayer, the Divine Office. The Divine Office is Christ at prayer in His Church. The Divine Office is recited by all priests, by most consecrated and religious, and by many lay persons. In it they unite themselves to Christ, praying as He did and for the purposes for which He prayed. Like Christ, they pray to give glory to God and to thank Him for His greatness and goodness,

to beg His pardon for sin and to offer reparation for it, and to gain graces and blessings for the entire human race. In the Divine Office, especially the Psalms, we join with Christ as He prays.

The Church, from day to day, from hour to hour, prays the Divine Office. Together with the Holy Sacrifice of the Mass, the prayers of the Divine Office are continually being raised up to God for every member of the Church, the Mystical Body of Christ.

The Divine Office unites us very closely with Christ and with all the members of His Mystical Body, offering prayer to God. It brings us closer to living in the true spirit of the Church Year.

The Divine Office and the Holy Sacrifice of the Mass are very closely related in the liturgy. The Divine Office prepares the setting for the Holy Sacrifice of the Mass. In this way the Divine Office serves the greatest act of the liturgy—the Holy Sacrifice of the Mass.

Referring to the Divine Office, Pius XI once said, "What a spectacle for heaven and earth is not the Church at prayer. For centuries without interruption, from midnight to midnight, the divine psalmody of the inspired canticles is repeated on earth."

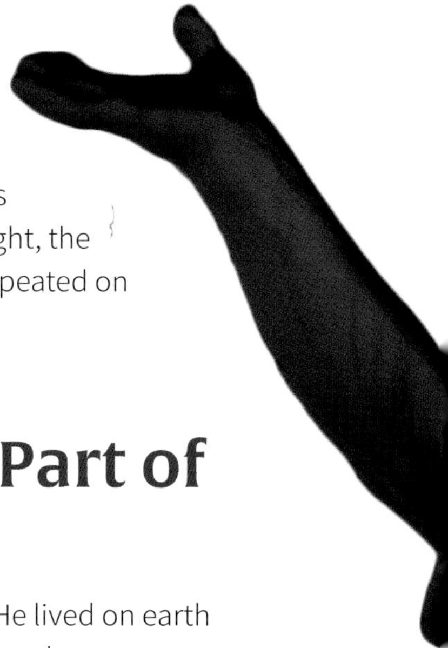

The Psalms—Chief Part of the Office

Before Jesus came and even during the time He lived on earth it was customary to pray psalms, for instance, at the ceremony of eating the Paschal Lamb. These psalms were hymns of praise glorifying God and thanking Him for His gifts, and especially for delivering the Israelites from Egypt.

Christ, together with His disciples, sang these psalms during the Great Passover before the institution of the Holy Eucharist on Holy Thursday.

When Jesus hung on the cross He used some of the psalms found in the Divine Office. Some of the last words spoken by Christ on the cross were words taken from Psalm 21, "My God, my God, why have you forsaken me?"

Jesus Himself recited the psalms. He continues reciting these beautiful praises with us in His Mystical Body, the Church.

One of the greatest writers of the psalms was David, the shepherd boy who later became king. David was very gifted in writing poetry and in playing the harp. While on the hillside tending his sheep David would write beautiful poems or verses about God. He would put these words to music and sing them.

Even as a king, David continued writing poems and putting them to music. These religious hymns or poems are called *Psalms.* Some of these poems foretold the Passion and resurrection of our Lord; others again are petitions to God for mercy.

> "The Lord has reigned, let the people be
> angry: he that sits on the cherubims: let the earth be moved.
> The Lord is great in Sion, and high
> above all people.
> Let them give praise to your great name:
> for it is terrible and holy."
>
> —Psalm 99 [98]:1–3

FOR ME TO REVIEW

Questions

1. What is the Divine Office?
2. Why is the Divine Office important in the liturgy?
3. What psalm did Christ recite before He died?
4. Who is the greatest writer of the Psalms?
5. What do you understand by the word *Psalms?*
6. How are the Holy Sacrifice of the Mass and the Divine Office related?

FOR ME TO REMEMBER

1. Prayer is the lifting up of our minds and hearts to God.
2. The Divine Office contains certain prayers, psalms, and hymns of praise, thanksgiving, reparation, and petition.
3. The Divine Office is recited by all priests. It is also said by many consecrated, religious, and lay persons.
4. When we say the Divine Office we join with Christ and His Church in praising God.
5. The Holy Sacrifice of the Mass and the Divine Office are closely united.
6. The Divine Office brings us closer to living in the true spirit of the Liturgical Year.
7. Psalms are religious hymns of praise, thanksgiving, petition, and reparation.
8. One of the greatest writers of the psalms was King David.

FOR ME TO DO

1. Set a psalm to music.
2. Make a bookmark. Print a quotation from one of David's psalms.
3. Memorize a few verses from one of David's psalms.
5. Recite or chant one of the following psalms before or at the closing of the lesson. Suggestions:

   Psalm 8, "O Lord, Our Lord, how glorious is Your Name."

   Psalm 22, "The Lord is my Shepherd."

   Psalm 129, "Out of the depths."

   Psalm 148, "Praise the Lord from the heavens."

   Psalm 150, "Praise the Lord in His sanctuary."

CHAPTER 10

The Sacraments

The sacraments are rivers of grace in which our Lord through His Mystical Body brings us divine life.

We know that Adam and Eve disobeyed God and lost the divine life of sanctifying grace. We know that they lost this holiness not only for themselves, but also for us, their children. By His suffering and death on the cross, Jesus won back this gift of grace for us.

Grace is a gift. Through it we share God's own life. It gives us new life and makes us adopted sons of God. Furthermore, grace helps us to act as Jesus Christ showed and taught us to act—to be good like Jesus, to be truthful like Jesus, to be loving like Jesus, to be strong as Jesus was in doing what is right, and to be self-controlled like Jesus.

Sanctifying grace *first, makes us holy and pleasing to God; second, makes us adopted children of God; third, makes us temples of the Holy Ghost; fourth,* ***enables us to live with God on earth and for eternity in heaven.***

Through the liturgy, God shares with us this divine life, that is, grace, which helps us to become Christlike. By doing this, Christ is not only helping us to become holy, but He is also giving honor and glory to His Father in heaven. He told St. Joseph and His Mother, the Blessed Virgin Mary, that they should not have worried about Him because He was "going about doing the work of His Father in heaven." Today Christ continues this work in the Church through the liturgy.

Christ wishes to give us many blessings through the liturgy. He tries to lead us to these gifts of grace. He does this by giving us signs which tell us what these graces are. These signs also help us know that we have received grace. These signs are the *sacraments,* which He instituted as part of the liturgy.

Christ gives His own divine power to the sacraments, and when we receive them, grace comes through Him to us, the members of His Mystical Body. A human body has its own means of providing for its life and health. For the Mystical Body, Christ, our Savior, provides means also. Each member is helped from birth to death by the sacraments.

The sacraments are like so many rivers through which our Lord brings us the wonderful life of grace. By examining each of the sacraments we can see how Christ shares His life with us.

Baptism—Gives Us Divine Life

Not long after Jesus began His public life, a certain rich man named Nicodemus came to see Him. Nicodemus wanted to find out if Jesus were truly the Messiah.

Jesus welcomed Nicodemus and explained to him how God so loved man that He sent His only-begotten Son to redeem the world. He then told Nicodemus what he should do to enter life everlasting. Christ said: ". . . unless a man be born again of water and the Spirit, he cannot enter into the kingdom of God" (Jn. 3:5).

When we receive Baptism we are re-born to a new life of grace, a Christ-life which enables us to act in a supernatural way. We are cleansed of original sin, and God Himself comes to live in us, giving us the power to act in a Godlike way. Heaven is once again opened to us.

The sacrament of Baptism is the first step we take in the life of the Church.

By the sacrament of Baptism we are cleansed of original sin and stamped with the seal of Christ. By it we are joined with Christ and made members of His Mystical Body on earth, the Church. Baptism gives us a share in Christ's saving work. The waters of baptism purify the soul. Water symbolizes life, as all living things need water to grow. But water also symbolizes death—consider the story of Noah and the Ark. When we are baptized, our old self is put to death, and we receive new life in Christ. In this sacrament we receive Christ's divine life, with new powers of the soul which help us reach heaven. These powers are faith, hope, and charity.

Supernatural faith helps us to believe firmly all the truths God has revealed. Supernatural hope enables us to trust God and depend upon Him for helping us to get to heaven. Supernatural charity helps us to love God and our neighbor as ourselves for the love of God.

Baptism makes us workers in Christ's Mystical Body. In order to live in accord with our baptismal promises, we must lovingly serve God and our neighbor. Christ has given us life and desires that we live it abundantly. The life of the Christian is unselfish. To give of ourselves is also to find ourselves, because in giving we become more like Christ in whose image we are made.

Confirmation—Strengthens Divine Life in Us

If you were asked, "What is a sacrament?" no doubt you would quickly answer: *A sacrament is an outward sign instituted by Christ to give grace.* We could say that the sacraments were instituted to make us holy, to lead us to God, and that they enable us to serve and worship God. Each sacrament that we receive aids us to belong more and more to Jesus Christ and to His Mystical Body, the Church.

The sacrament of Baptism is the entrance door to Christ's Church on earth. It gives us sanctifying grace. The sacrament of Confirmation strengthens the life of sanctifying grace in us.

Confirmation is the sacrament through which the Holy Ghost comes to us in a special way to enable us to profess our faith as strong and perfect Christians and soldiers of Jesus Christ.

Confirmation gives us a new work to do in the Mystical Body of Christ. We must help bishops and priests help others. This sacrament gives us strength to do it. A soldier has the privilege and duty to serve his country and to defend it. Confirmed members of the Mystical Body have the power and the duty to work with the Holy Father and bishops. They must help the Church and defend it against its enemies.

The Holy Spirit changes us when we receive the sacrament. We are no longer regular members of the Mystical Body of Christ, but we become defenders of that great body. We become better able to live our faith with courage. In order to act as good members a special grace is needed. We get this grace and strength at Confirmation.

In Confirmation the Holy Spirit comes to us in a special manner with His seven gifts: wisdom, which gives us a desire for the things of God and act so that we give Him honor and glory;

understanding, which helps us to know more clearly the mysteries of our faith; counsel, which warns us against the devil and dangers to supernatural life; fortitude, which strengthens us to do the will of God in all things; knowledge, which helps us to discover the will of God in all things; piety, which helps us to love God as a Father and obey Him because we love Him; fear of the Lord, which fills us with hatred for sin.

Like the sacrament of Baptism, Confirmation marks us with the seal of Christ. These spiritual marks can never be erased. They will remain on our souls for all eternity.

Now we can see how another sacrament is used as a part of the liturgy in order to help us grow in holiness and become more Christlike.

Holy Eucharist—Increases Divine Life in Us

In the Holy Eucharist, the greatest of all the sacraments, Christ, the Head of the Mystical Body, and we the members, become very closely united. We grow in love for Him and for one another.

The organs and members of our natural bodies need food to grow and become strong. The same is true of the members of the Mystical Body of Christ. They need spiritual food to give them energy to grow and become strong in the divine life. That is why, in the Holy Eucharist, Christ, the Head of the Mystical Body, offers Himself as a divine food to us, the members of this Body. By eating this heavenly food, the Holy Eucharist, we grow and become strong with the strength and the virtues of Christ.

In all the other sacraments we share Christ's holy life; in this one we actually receive Christ Himself—His body, blood, soul, and divinity. This is the great work of the liturgy through which Christ makes us like Himself.

> *"There is nothing so great as the Eucharist. If God had something more precious He would have given it to us."*
>
> *—St. John Vianney*

Through the Blessed Eucharist, Christ Himself can make our wills like His Will. By uniting ourselves to Him at Communion, we can love God and our fellow men just as Christ does. The Eucharist purifies our desires. When we receive Holy Communion, we come to love the things of God. Holy Communion is not meant only for ourselves. When we receive Holy Communion, we unite ourselves with the whole world, because we are united with its maker: God. We do not know how God will use the graces that come from our worthy reception of the Blessed Sacrament. But we trust that He will use all things for the good of those who love Him.

The Holy Eucharist keeps the Mystical Body of Christ, the Church, alive. It has in itself the very life of God. This sacrament can make a great change in our lives, for by it Christ Himself lives in us and we in Him. Through the liturgy Christ is still working to save men. We can see, then, how the Holy Eucharist is a great blessing and privilege.

Penance and Reconciliation—Increases or Restores Divine Life in Us

We have learned that Baptism is our first great step in the life of the Church. By it Christ makes us members of His Mystical Body and we are thus enabled to enter the kingdom of heaven. However, we must co-operate with Christ, our Head, in His great work of salvation if we hope to experience the joy of Eternal Life. Since Christ knew that some of His members would fall into sin, He made it possible for them to receive forgiveness through the sacrament of Penance and Reconciliation.

This sacrament is a very important part of the liturgy. Christ uses this sacrament to reunite us to Himself if we have cut ourselves off from Him by committing serious sin.

In the sacrament of Penance and Reconciliation Christ forgives us our sins and also removes part of the punishment due to venial sin. He makes us strong and helps us to defend ourselves against sin.

The sacrament of Penance and Reconciliation is a rich treasure house. We come to it in sorrow and sin, and leave without them. We carry away God's treasures of forgiveness, sanctifying grace, remission of punishment, help for the future, and credit for the past.

Christ wants us to be living members of His Mystical Body. In His great mercy, He looks for the sinner who has become a weak member of that Body. Through Penance and Reconciliation the member is restored to supernatural life and made strong and active again.

Truly, we can say that the sacrament of Penance and Reconciliation is a great gift to the Church. In it we find Jesus still forgiving us every time we are sorry, and leading us on to heaven with the graces this great sacrament supplies.

Holy Orders—Sharing in Christ's Priesthood

In studying the sacrament of Baptism we discovered that we not only share in the life of Christ; in a certain sense we also take part in the priesthood of Christ and in Christ's priestly work of giving glory to God by helping men to be like God. We will understand this more clearly when we study the Holy Sacrifice of the Mass. All the members of Christ's Mystical Body share this privilege, but some become priests in the full sense.

This is reserved to a special group whom Christ chooses to be "other Christs." They receive the priesthood in the sacrament of Holy Orders. By this sacrament Christ gives priests the power to offer the great Sacrifice of the Mass, which gives so much glory to God. By it He also gives them the power to administer sacraments and to teach and preach the word of God. In other words, priests are to do the work which Christ Himself started on earth and which the Apostles continued after His ascension into heaven.

The priests and bishops are only taking Christ's place when they give us the sacraments. As members of the Mystical Body of Christ, they supply the voice, the actions, and take the place of Christ. They are only His agents, His ministers. And the divine life which is given us is not theirs. It is Christ's life.

To help us understand what the sacrament of Holy Orders has to do with our supernatural life, this comparison might help. We know that there is such a thing as electricity. It can be used in many ways if the switch is turned on. So, too, with our divine life. The sacraments are sources of divine life, but we need someone to bring this life to us and to make it grow stronger. Holy Orders gives priests the power to bring supernatural life to us. It gives them the ability to do Christ's work, the great work of giving God glory and bringing men to heaven. They, as it were, turn the switch.

Matrimony—Foreshadows the Mystical Body of Christ

St. Paul called the sacrament of Matrimony a "great mystery." In this sacrament two Catholics bind themselves to live together as husband and wife. They promise to live with one another and to love one another until they die. This sacrament gives them the ability to co-operate with God in bringing children into the world and in rearing them as good Catholics.

By the sacrament of Matrimony Christ gives the two people who receive it the graces they need to make their marriage happy, holy, and fruitful. They also receive grace which helps them faithfully to perform their duties toward one another and toward their children.

Like the other sacraments, Matrimony is also part of the liturgical life of the Church. It is a sacrament which blesses husband and wife, uniting the love they have for each other to God's love. St. Paul said that the love between husband and wife is like Christ's love for His Church. Through the sacrament of Matrimony two members of Christ's Mystical Body are specially blessed. They can offer their children to Christ as new members of His Mystical Body.

Anointing of the Sick—the Last "Anointing"

From the day of our baptism until death, the Church, like a loving Mother, nourishes and guards the Christ-life in us. Often during our lives we receive the sacrament of Holy Eucharist by which we become closely united to Christ and to one another. In the sacrament of Confirmation the Holy Spirit made us strong defenders of the Mystical Body. If we ever separate ourselves from Christ by grievous sin, we can once more become His friends by receiving the sacrament of Penance and Reconciliation. All through our earthly life we live with, through, and in Christ until we reach the last moment when we are ready to take our final step toward eternity.

Since the moment of death is very important, Christ has given us another sacrament to help us at that time. This is the sacrament of Anointing of the Sick. In it Christ cleanses us from the remains of sin, strengthens us for our last journey, and prepares us to enter His heavenly Father's Kingdom.

FOR ME TO REVIEW

Catechism Lesson

601. **Q. Besides sanctifying grace, do the sacraments give any other grace?**
A. Besides sanctifying grace, the sacraments give another grace, called sacramental grace.

602. **Q. What is sacramental grace?**
A. Sacramental grace is a special help which God gives, to attain the end for which He instituted each sacrament.

605. **Q. Do the sacraments always give grace?**
A. The sacraments always give grace, if we receive them with the right dispositions.

621. **Q. What is Baptism?**
A. Baptism is a sacrament which cleanses us from original sin, makes us Christians, children of God, and heirs of heaven.

670. **Q. What is Confirmation?**
A. Confirmation is a sacrament through which we receive the Holy Ghost to make us strong and perfect Christians and soldiers of Jesus Christ.

870. **Q. What is the Holy Eucharist?**
A. The Holy Eucharist is the sacrament which contains the Body and Blood, Soul and Divinity, of our Lord Jesus Christ under the appearances of bread and wine.

873. **Q. When did Christ institute the Holy Eucharist?**
A. Christ instituted the Holy Eucharist at the Last Supper, the night before He died.

898. **Q. What is Holy Communion?**
A. Holy Communion is the receiving of the Body and Blood of Christ.

721. **Q. What is the sacrament of Penance and Reconciliation?**
A. Penance and Reconciliation is a sacrament in which the sins committed after Baptism are forgiven.

956. **Q. What is the sacrament of Anointing of the Sick?**
A. Anointing of the Sick is the sacrament which, through the anointing and prayer of the priest, gives health and strength to the soul, and sometimes to the body, when we are in danger of death from sickness.

978. **Q. What is the sacrament of Holy Orders?**
A. Holy Orders is a sacrament by which bishops, priests, and other ministers of the Church are ordained and receive the power and grace to perform their sacred duties.

1005. **Q. What is the sacrament of Matrimony?**
A. The sacrament of Matrimony is the sacrament which unites a Christian man and woman in lawful marriage.

Questions

Answer yes or no.

1. Is "supernatural life" the same as "divine life"?
2. Do all sacraments give divine life?
3. Is supernatural life a gift of God which allows us to share in His own life?
4. Does Baptism make us members of Christ's Church on earth?
5. Are all sins taken away by Baptism?
6. Do the words "to be born of water and the Holy Spirit" refer to Baptism?
7. Is it necessary that every adult Catholic be confirmed?
8. Does the sacrament of Confirmation help us to practice our faith?

9. Will receiving Holy Communion often make us more Christlike?
10. Is Christ really present in the Holy Eucharist?
11. Is the Holy Eucharist a sacrament?
12. Did Christ mean what He said: "Take and eat; this is my Body"?
13. Was the sacrament of Penance and Reconciliation instituted to give back divine life if it is lost through mortal sin?
14. Does Penance and Reconciliation increase sanctifying grace?
15. Are all priests "other Christs"?
16. May all people receive the sacrament of Holy Orders?
17. May a person who has already died receive Anointing of the Sick?
18. Must all sacraments be received in the state of grace?
19. Are the sacraments a part of the sacred liturgy?
20. Do all sacraments mark our souls with the seal of Christ?

FOR ME TO REMEMBER

1. Sacraments are outward signs which give us grace and show us that Christ is at work within us.
2. Sacraments are ways through which we gain or receive an increase of sanctifying grace and of sacramental graces.
3. In Baptism we are stamped with the seal of Christ and made members of His Mystical Body.
4. Baptism is the beginning of our supernatural life.
5. In Confirmation the Holy Spirit lives in us in a special way.
6. The sacrament of Confirmation strengthens the Christ-life in us.

7. There are seven gifts of the Holy Spirit.
8. The Holy Eucharist is a sacrifice and a sacrament.
9. Christ instituted the Holy Eucharist in order to unite Himself closely with all the members of His Mystical Body.
10. The sacrament of Penance and Reconciliation was instituted by Christ to bring back supernatural life if we lose it through sin.
11. Penance and Reconciliation is a sacrament of the dead, that is, of those who have deprived themselves of sanctifying grace.
12. Christ instituted the sacrament of Penance and Reconciliation chiefly to take away mortal sin, which kills the life of grace in our souls.
13. Christ instituted the sacrament of Holy Orders at the Last Supper.
14. The sacrament of Holy Orders gives priests the power to continue the work which Christ did when He was on earth.
15. Priests are "other Christs" who have the power to impart to us divine life.
16. Matrimony is a sacrament through which God unites a man and woman for life and blesses their love for one another.
17. Anointing of the Sick prepares us for our entrance into eternity.
18. Anointing of the Sick gives health and strength to our soul.

FOR ME TO DO

1. Draw symbols for each of the seven sacraments.
2. Make a Sacrament Book. In it have pictures, stories, poems, and prayers about the various sacraments showing how Christ gives His divine life through them.
3. Make a list of things which Christ does for us in Baptism, and tell why each is important.
4. Watch a Baptism. Prepare a short reflection on the ceremony.
5. Compose an original prayer to the Holy Spirit asking Him for the seven gifts.
6. Write a short paragraph telling what Christ in the Holy Eucharist does for you.
7. In connection with the sacrament of Penance and Reconciliation illustrate either of the Bible stories—the Prodigal Son or The Good Shepherd.
8. Prepare a discussion on "Why we should show great love and respect for priests."
9. Give examples of how you can practice your faith as a strong and perfect Christian and soldier of Jesus Christ.
10. Write a letter to your friend telling why it is important to receive the sacrament of Anointing of the Sick while we are still conscious, that is, while we still know what is going on.

CHAPTER 11
Sacramentals

When Christ lived on earth He used creatures to help Him do His work among men. He used water and the dust of the earth to heal people. When He cured the man born blind, He "spread the clay over his eyes . . ." Then He told the man to "wash in the pool of Siloam" (Jn. 9:6, 7). Along with the gift of sight the man received the gift of faith.

Today Christ continues to live among us in His Mystical Body, the Church. He uses created objects to be the great channels of grace in the sacraments. He also allows the Church to bless many things of the earth to help us gain graces to incite good thoughts and increase devotion and thus preserve us or cleanse us from venial sin. These holy things are called *sacramentals.* They do not give grace by themselves. But, if properly used, they prepare us to receive sanctifying grace.

Mother Church asks God to give her members certain helps when they use the sacramentals in the proper way, with faith and devotion. God sends His helps through the Church to us, its members.

Since all creation is the work of God, and since the earth has been especially blessed because Christ lived on it, all things should be a means of leading us to heaven. Every creature can become for us, as it were, a sacramental.

The crucifix, for example, reminds us of the Passion and death of our Lord Jesus Christ. It helps to arouse in us a deep love for our Savior, gratitude for His goodness, a sincere sorrow for our sins, and a strong will not to sin again. This special help is

supernatural because it comes from God and is called *actual grace*—one of the most important favors or gifts of the sacramentals.

Another example of a sacramental is the sign of the cross. Through this sign, we unite ourselves to the most Holy Trinity. After the sign of the cross, the sacramental most often used is holy water. Holy water helps us to recall our baptism and our calling as children of God.

> "Sacramentals do not confer the grace of the Holy Spirit in the way that the sacraments do, but by the Church's prayer, they prepare us to receive grace and dispose us to cooperate with it."
>
> —Catechism of the Catholic Church, 1670

Other sacramentals are blessed candles, ashes, palms, statues of our Lord, of the Blessed Virgin and of the saints, rosaries, medals, and many other things.

Besides objects, certain actions are considered sacramentals.

When Jesus was on earth He blessed people. Christ wants us to have His blessing today just as He wanted the people of long ago to have it.

The Church has many blessings for people and for things. She blesses churches, schools, homes, indeed any building. She blesses the sick, children, mothers. She blesses crops, ships, airplanes, automobiles. All these and many other blessings are sacramentals.

The sacramentals are different from the sacraments. Jesus gave us the sacraments. The Church gives us the sacramentals. There are seven sacraments but there are hundreds of sacramentals. The sacraments give grace directly but the sacramentals are only helps to grace.

Sacramentals are means Christ uses to show His love for us. They are ways by which He draws us to Himself. Christ shows His goodness in every need of our lives through the liturgy, which is His work in the Church.

FOR ME TO REVIEW

Catechism Lesson

1052. Q. What is a sacramental?

A. A sacramental is anything set apart or blessed by the Church to excite good thoughts and to increase devotion, and through these movements of the heart to remit venial sin.

1063. Q. Which is the chief sacramental used in the Church?

A. The chief sacramental used in the Church is the sign of the cross.

1074. Q. Are there other sacramentals besides the sign of the cross and holy water?

A. Beside the sign of the cross and holy water there are many other sacramentals, such as blessed candles, ashes, palms, crucifixes, images of the Blessed Virgin and of the saints, rosaries, and scapulars.

Questions

1. What is a sacramental?
2. List some of the most widely used sacramentals. Tell how each helps us receive grace.
3. What is the chief difference between the sacraments and the sacramentals?
4. Who gave us the sacramentals?

FOR ME TO REMEMBER

1. Sacramentals are holy things or actions blessed by the Church to obtain for us spiritual and temporal favors.
2. Sacramentals were instituted by the Church to help us gain grace.

FOR ME TO DO

1. Make a diagram showing the chief differences between the sacraments and the sacramentals.
2. List all the sacramentals you can find in your home. Share with others how they can help you.

CHAPTER 12
The Liturgical Year or the Church Year

The Meaning of the Church Year

It was the first Sunday in Advent. The priest announced from the pulpit that on this day the Catholic Church begins a new year—a year known as the Church Year or Liturgical Year.

What is the Church Year?

When we think of a "year" we usually have in mind the year that begins on January 1 and ends December 31. This is the year which is made up of 365 days, 52 weeks, 12 months, and 4 seasons. During it we celebrate numerous holidays, such as Thanksgiving, July 4, Labor Day, etc., to recall important events that took place in our country, and to keep alive the memory of those who helped make our country great.

The Church has its own year, called the Church Year or the Liturgical Year. Like the ordinary year, the Liturgical Year is also divided into periods of time. In each of these periods the important events in the life of Christ, of His mother, and of His saints are celebrated by the Church. These events remind us of our redemption, and help us come closer to Christ. The ordinary year has four equal seasons. In the Church Year, however, there are only two seasons, and they are not equally divided, as are the seasons of the ordinary year. The first of these two seasons of the Church Year is centered around Christmas and reminds us that God the Son became man; the other, which is much longer, is centered around Easter and around the work of Christ in redeeming man.

Division of the Ecclesiastical Year

Ordinary Form

Christmas Cycle

Period	Time
1. Advent	First Sunday of Advent to December 24
2. Christmas	December 24 to the Baptism of our Lord
3. Ordinary Time	Baptism of our Lord to Ash Wednesday

Easter Cycle

Period	Time
1. Lent	Ash Wednesday to Easter Sunday
Holy Week	Palm Sunday to Easter Sunday
2. Easter	Easter Sunday to Pentecost
3. Ordinary Time	Pentecost to Advent

Extraordinary Form

The extraordinary form of the Mass adheres to the 1962 liturgical calendar. It differs from the liturgical calendar of the ordinary form of the Mass in many small ways. The extraordinary form has a season before Lent called Septuagesima, which the calendar of the ordinary form does not include.

Christmas Cycle

Period	Time
1. Advent	First Sunday of Advent to December 24
2. Christmastide	December 24 to January 14
Christmastide Proper	December 24 to January 6
Season of Epiphany	January 6 to January 14
3. Time after Epiphany	January 14 to Septuagesima Sunday

Easter Cycle

Period	Time
1. Septuagesima	Septuagesima Sunday to Ash Wednesday
2. Lent	Ash Wednesday to Easter Sunday
Lenten Season	Ash Wednesday to First Passion Sunday
Passiontide	Passion Sunday to Easter Sunday
3. Eastertide	Easter Sunday to Trinity Sunday
Eastertide Proper	Easter Sunday to Ascension
Ascensiontide	Ascension to Pentecost Sunday
Octave of Pentecost	Pentecost Sunday to Trinity Sunday
4. Time after Pentecost	Trinity Sunday to Advent

In the calendar of the ordinary form, the readings change according to a three-year cycle: A, B, and C. Unlike the extraordinary form, where there is only one cycle of readings, the readings for the calendar of the ordinary form are selected according to the three-year cycle.

The Liturgical Year begins with *Advent,* which is the first part of the Christmas season. Advent falls at the end of November or early December, *as winter approaches,* and when the days are short and cold and dark. The sun drops to its lowest point and all nature seems dead. The flowers have withered, the trees have shed their leaves, and most of the birds have left us. This gives us a picture of fallen man before the coming of our Lord. Because of sin people wait for the Redeemer in deep spiritual darkness. Then Christ arrives!

In the liturgy each year when the days are just beginning to get longer, Christ, the Light of the World, comes like the rising sun to overcome the darkness of sin and death. The sun gives warmth to the earth; without this warmth there could be no life. In a similar manner Christ, the divine Son, sends out the rays of His life-giving warmth of grace to the whole world. Christ said of Himself: "I am the light of the world" (Jn. 8:12). "I came that they may have life" (Jn. 10:10).

Lent, the first part of the Easter season, *comes as spring approaches.* There are days in this season when it rains and shines at one and the same time. This is a picture of winter and spring struggling with each other. The battle between spring and winter helps us to understand our Lord's fighting with death, sin, and darkness of mind. By Easter He has conquered! Then the Winter of Sin has gone and the Spring of Grace is here.

The season of *Pentecost,* the coming of the Holy Spirit, which is part of the Church's Easter season, *begins as summer draws near,* and lasts throughout the summer and fall. Through the long days of summer and the early autumn the blossoms change into fruit. So, too, the life and grace which Christ brought to earth brings forth spiritual fruit in men.

So you see, in the Liturgical Year as in the ordinary year, there is a beginning of life, early growth in the spring, a ripening in the summer, a harvest in the autumn.

The events in our Lord's life are arranged in the order in which the Church thinks about and celebrates them, with one thing happening after another almost as it did when our Lord was on earth. In this way Christ Himself continues to live in His Church in order that we might stay close to His mysteries and, in a way, live through them with Him.

The life of Christ in the liturgy is like a great drama or a holy play. Christ allows us to act His part with Him as He again lives through the many events of His life. We also follow the lives of the

Blessed Virgin Mary, the angels, and the saints as they show us how to honor God by living like His divine Son.

It is the Liturgical Year that helps us to live this sacred drama of the life of Christ, a drama which begins with the promise of a Redeemer in the Garden of Eden and ends only on the day of judgment. We are not only an audience in this drama; we take part in it just as actors do in a play. More than that, we give our minds, our hearts, our bodies, our wills, everything we have and are to Christ.

He unites us to Himself, and together with us He re-lives His holy life and death. We are born with Him at Christmas. We walk up and down the Holy Land with Him doing good, only now the Holy Land is our own country. We offer ourselves with Him to His heavenly Father in the Passion, and we arise with Him in glory on Easter. We ascend with Him into heaven and we share in the great work of Christ in His Church. Christ works to sanctify and save men. We work in and with Him, in our own parish, in our own country, in our world.

The Liturgical Year is not just a time to recall events long past. It is a period to re-live each event and act in the life of Christ, and to imitate the virtues of the saints. It is for each one of us a re-living of a Christ-life, a holy life, a life of grace.

The Liturgical Year is sometimes called the *year of grace* because Christ Himself is with us at each feast during the year. It keeps Christ living in our minds and hearts. The events in our Lord's life did not happen only in the past, they are not done and over with. Christ is continually being born again in our hearts through sanctifying grace. Every day is a day of our Risen, Glorious, and Ascended Christ, who is the Head of the Mystical Body of which we are the members. The Holy Spirit is continually coming down to live in us. In the Liturgical Year we live these events over again and gain great spiritual benefit from them.

> *"In the liturgical year the various aspects of the one Paschal mystery unfold."*
>
> —*Catechism of the Catholic Church, 1171*

The Church Year and Its Graces

At each event in His life, and in every mystery, Christ gained special graces for us. He won these graces in His infancy, in His hidden life, in His public life, in His sufferings and death, in His Resurrection and glorious Ascension, and in His sending the Holy Spirit.

Advent bestows on us patience. Christmas brings us love; Epiphany wakens in us the spirit of respect toward Christ, our King. Lent gives us the spirit of penance, patience in suffering, and hatred for sin. Easter fills our souls with the joy of victory over death.

The Liturgical Year not only teaches us the great truths about our Savior; it shows us a way of living closely united with Him and with each other.

It offers us a chance to feel with Christ and the Church, to think as Christ and the Church thinks, to act as Christ and the Church would have us act. It makes us all one with Christ in His Mystical Body, the Church.

FOR ME TO REVIEW

Questions

1. What is the Liturgical Year?
2. When does the Liturgical Year begin?
3. Name the main seasons of the Liturgical Year.
4. How can we share in the life of Christ?
5. Which is the best way to honor God?
6. Compare the Liturgical Year with the ordinary year and show in which ways they are alike.

FOR ME TO REMEMBER

1. The Liturgical Year is Christ re-living His life to share it with us.
2. Christmas and Easter are the two main seasons of the Church Year.
3. The Liturgical Year begins with the first Sunday of Advent and ends with the thirty-fourth week of Ordinary Time (ordinary form) or last week after Pentecost (extraordinary form).

FOR ME TO DO

1. Make a wall chart illustrating the two divisions of the Liturgical Year. Fill in the principal feasts in the life of Christ during each of these periods.
2. Find or draw pictures of the seasons in the ordinary year. By means of a diagram illustrate how the Liturgical Year fits into the pattern of the ordinary year.

Summary of Unit 3

The liturgy is the exterior and interior worship we give to God. It is the act of Christ, as Head of His Mystical Body, adoring and thanking His heavenly Father, making up for the sins of men, and bringing down God's blessings upon them.

We become Christ's members through the sacrament of baptism. The other sacraments either increase Christ's life in us or, if we have lost it through sin, restore us to it. The sacraments belong to the liturgy because in them Christ acts through His Church and gives grace.

The central act of the liturgy is the Mass, for here Christ is both victim and priest, and in the Mass He renews in an unblood way the sacrifice of the cross.

We re-live, through the liturgy, the life of Christ. Centered around the two seasons of Christmas and Easter, the liturgy give us Christ: first, as promised to the people of the Old Testament; next, as the God-Man, the child of Mary who lived and died in Palestine; finally, as the glorious King who will come to judge all men at the end of the world.

O Quam Suavis Est

O how sweet, Lord, is your Spirit! That you may manifest your sweetness to your children, may you fill up with all good things those hungering for the sweet Bread come down from heaven, bestowing abundant riches upon the weak.

Write your answers on a separate sheet of paper

Part 1 True-False

1. Psalms are sacred songs or poems.
2. Using sacramentals is a means to make us more pleasing to God.
3. In the sacrifice of the Mass Christ is both priest and victim.
4. The Liturgical Year begins on Christmas Day.
5. In the sacraments of Baptism and Confirmation the Holy Spirit comes to dwell in us.
6. Living the liturgy means living with Christ, His Blessed Mother, and the saints in the Church.
7. God gives us actual grace each time we receive the sacraments worthily.
8. Priests are required to recite the Divine Office every day.

Part 2 Completion

Use the following words to complete the sentences below.

Divine Office	sacramental	Last Supper
psalms	Penance and Reconciliation	sanctifying grace
suffering	missal	Mass
knowledge		

1. When we were baptized we became rich with. . . . . . .
2. Our Lord merited many graces for us through His. . . . . . .
3. If we have lost the love of God through sin we should receive the sacrament of. . . . . . .
4. Jesus offered the first Mass at the. . . . . . .

5. Blessed palms and holy water are called. . . . . . .
6. The highest form of worship is the. . . . . . .
7. The book that contains all the prayers used at Mass is the. . . . . . .
8. The gift of the Holy Spirit which helps us discover the will of God is. . . . . . .
9. The official daily prayer of the Church is. . . . . . .
10. Hymns of praise glorifying and thanking God for His gifts are. . . . . . .

Part 3 Multiple Choice

Choose the one answer that makes each sentence correct.

1. The best way to obtain grace is:
   A. to pray and receive the sacraments.
   B. to go to a Catholic school.
   C. to speak kindly of others.
2. Living with Christ in the Church is called:
   A. the Mystical Body.
   B. the liturgy.
   C. the Missal.
3. By divine faith we believe:
   A. all that God has revealed to us.
   B. anything a priest tells us.
   C. just what is in the Bible.
4. We best prove that we love God when:
   A. we obey His commandments.
   B. we go to Mass.
   C. we just tell Him we love Him.

5. The sacrament by which Christ prepares us for death and
   A. heaven is:
   B. Baptism.
   C. Confirmation.
   D. Anointing of the Sick.

Part 4 Matching

Match each item in Column A with an item in Column B.

COLUMN A	COLUMN B
1. Grace that makes us holy and pleasing to God	A. to adore, ask, thank, and make up for sins
2. Principal ways of obtaining grace	B. sacraments
3. A supernatural help to do good and avoid evil	C. Holy Orders
4. Reasons for offering sacrifice	D. Christmas and Easter
5. Lifting of the heart and mind to God	E. David
6. The sacrament through which a man becomes a priest	F. prayer and sacraments
7. Seven means instituted by Christ to give grace	G. sanctifying grace
8. The main seasons of the Church Year	H. Baptism
9. Composed many psalms and set them to music	I. actual grace
10. The sacrament that serves as a gateway to a life of grace	J. prayer

All the good works in the world are not equal to the Holy Sacrifice of the Mass because they are the works of men; but the Mass is the work of God. Martyrdom is nothing in comparison for it is but the sacrifice of man to God; but the Mass is the sacrifice of God for man.

ST. JOHN VIANNEY

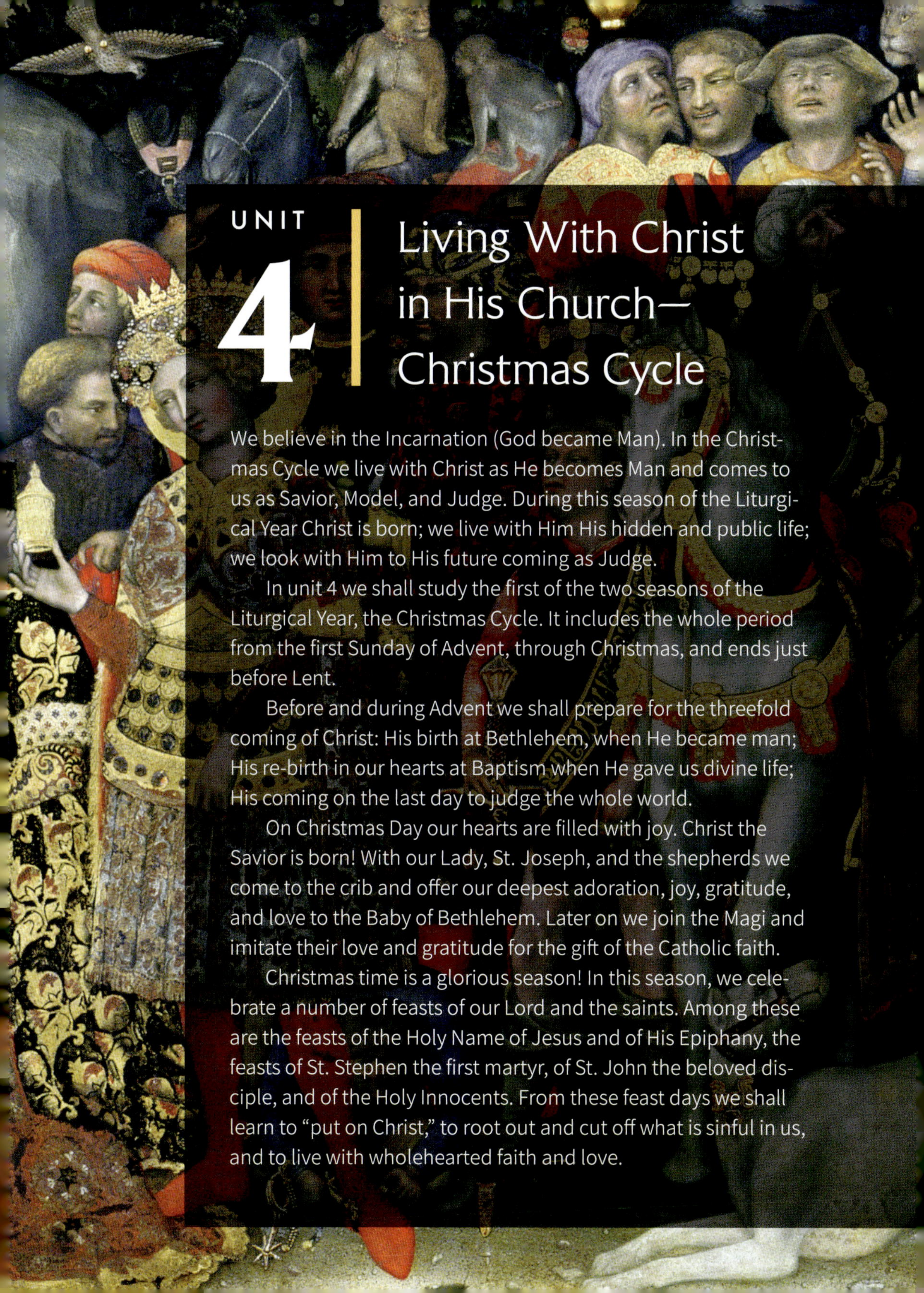

UNIT 4 | Living With Christ in His Church—Christmas Cycle

We believe in the Incarnation (God became Man). In the Christmas Cycle we live with Christ as He becomes Man and comes to us as Savior, Model, and Judge. During this season of the Liturgical Year Christ is born; we live with Him His hidden and public life; we look with Him to His future coming as Judge.

In unit 4 we shall study the first of the two seasons of the Liturgical Year, the Christmas Cycle. It includes the whole period from the first Sunday of Advent, through Christmas, and ends just before Lent.

Before and during Advent we shall prepare for the threefold coming of Christ: His birth at Bethlehem, when He became man; His re-birth in our hearts at Baptism when He gave us divine life; His coming on the last day to judge the whole world.

On Christmas Day our hearts are filled with joy. Christ the Savior is born! With our Lady, St. Joseph, and the shepherds we come to the crib and offer our deepest adoration, joy, gratitude, and love to the Baby of Bethlehem. Later on we join the Magi and imitate their love and gratitude for the gift of the Catholic faith.

Christmas time is a glorious season! In this season, we celebrate a number of feasts of our Lord and the saints. Among these are the feasts of the Holy Name of Jesus and of His Epiphany, the feasts of St. Stephen the first martyr, of St. John the beloved disciple, and of the Holy Innocents. From these feast days we shall learn to "put on Christ," to root out and cut off what is sinful in us, and to live with wholehearted faith and love.

CHAPTER 13 Preparing for the Coming of Christ in Time and in Eternity

God's Preparation of the World

When God drove Adam and Eve out of the Garden of Eden, they were very sad. Because of their sin of disobedience they had lost their perfect friendship with God. They had lost sanctifying grace, isolating themselves from God and from each other. And not only they, but all mankind, had to suffer because of their sins.

Adam and Eve were very unhappy because they knew they were unable to make amends to God for their great sin. Do you think there was any hope of forgiveness for Adam and Eve and their children? Before they were forced to leave the garden, but after they had sinned, God immediately showed his redeeming love for Adam and Eve by making them clothes (from animal skin) and covering the shame of their nakedness. This event hints at the "covering" of Adam and Eve's sinfulness through God's gift. Thus, God's mercy towards our first parents prefigures the perfect atonement that comes ultimately only by the blood of Christ. Before closing the gates of Paradise, God promised Adam and Eve that He would send a Redeemer who would break the power of the devil and give everyone a way to join Him in heaven.

God loved our first parents dearly. Do you think He could love all of us less than He loved Adam and Eve? No! God loved all men so much that He wanted all of them to become His children by grace. In His great love and goodness He planned a way by which He might regain for us a share in His divine life. He loved us so

much that He willed to send His own divine Son as a Redeemer to make up for the sin of our first parents and all of their children.

God knew how weak man was! He knew how quickly man would forget God. Hence, from time to time, He repeated the promise of the coming Redeemer; He told men things about the Redeemer that would help them know Him when He came. This promise of a Redeemer was repeated to certain chosen people of the Old Testament. We all remember Noah, Abraham, Isaac, Jacob, Judah, and David. What promise did God make to these friends of His? When did He make these promises? All of these friends of God lived a long time before Christ came, and during these many years God was preparing His people for the greatest event in the history of the world—the coming of the Savior, Jesus Christ.

The Prophets

As time went on, God raised among His Chosen People some good and holy men whom we know as *prophets.* Usually, when we think of prophets, we think of men who tell about future events. It is true that some of the Old Testament prophets told many things about the coming of a Redeemer. This was, however, only one part of their work. To *prophesy* means to speak in the name of another, and by the power of another. The prophets spoke for God. They reminded the people of their duty to God, and His goodness to them. They also told where the Redeemer would be born, what He would do, and what kind of life He would live. They also foretold that Christ would suffer and die for our sins, and that He would finally rise from the dead.

> *"And all the nations of the earth shall be blessed in him [Abraham]" (Gen. 18:18).*

Advent reminds us of the long period that the Israelites, the Chosen People of Old Testament times, waited for the coming of Christ. Just as the Chosen People were longing for the Promised Redeemer and preparing themselves for His coming, so we, too, prepare for the coming of the Christ Child on Christmas morn by doing little acts of sacrifice. We should cleanse ourselves from the least stain of sin in the sacrament of Penance and Reconciliation—the great sacrament of love and mercy. St. John the Baptist, the forerunner of Christ, and Mary Immaculate are our best helpers in preparing for the coming Redeemer. St. John the Baptist urges us to "make straight the way of the Lord" and Mary teaches us that our hearts must be immaculate, that is, free from every stain of sin. With them we shall prepare for and await the coming of the Savior.

How happy would the Chosen People have been if they could have lived with us in the Kingdom of Christ.

Mary's Preparation

At last God's promise of a Redeemer was to come true! Jesus the God-Man was to be born! He was to live on earth, to suffer, and to die to save us from sin.

Mary was chosen by God to be the Mother of His divine Son. From all eternity He prepared Mary for this great privilege. He filled her with divine love and grace and kept her free from any stain of sin.

One day the angel Gabriel appeared to the Blessed Virgin and said, "Hail, full of grace, the Lord is with thee. Blessed art thou among women" (Lk. 1:27).

When Mary heard the angel she was troubled, and wondered what these words meant.

"And the angel said to her, 'Do not be afraid, Mary, for thou hast found grace with God. Behold, thou shalt conceive in thy womb and shalt bring forth a son and thou shalt call his name Jesus'" (Lk. 1:30–31).

The Blessed Virgin Mary always wanted to do the will of God. She made it clear to the angel that if God wanted her to become the mother of His divine Son she was happy and very willing to do so. She replied, "Behold the handmaid of the Lord; be it done to me according to thy word" (Lk. 1:38).

We can learn from our Lady how we should prepare for the coming of our Savior, by prayer and by doing what God wants us to do. We should thank Mary for consenting to become the mother of Jesus and for playing such an important part in our redemption.

Our Preparation for the Coming of Christ

Just as the Jews of long ago yearned and prepared for the coming of the Redeemer, so during Advent we long for the coming of Christ on Christmas Night. Throughout Advent the Church in her prayers repeats: "He is coming! Christ is coming!"

Advent is a time of penance and prayer. St. John the Baptist and our Immaculate Mother can be our models during this time, when we must repent of our sins and the sins of others.

To find out the best way to spend Advent ask the Blessed Mother for help. It was she who brought Jesus into the world on a night many years ago. It is she who can teach us best how to bring Jesus into our hearts, how to be born again in the divine life, how to re-live with Him and her those sacred events as they are celebrated by the Church in the liturgy.

Jesus Christ helps us to prepare for His coming on Christmas Day. He likewise helps us get ready for His coming at the last judgment. In the Gospel we get a good picture of the end of the world. Christ warns us to live a true Christian life, to work with His graces, and to avoid sin in order to prepare for His coming as Judge and Savior.

FOR ME TO REVIEW

Questions

1. Why did God send His divine Son to earth?
2. How did Adam and Eve know that a Redeemer was to come?
3. Who is a prophet?
4. In what ways does the Blessed Virgin show us how to prepare for Christmas?
5. How does St. John the Baptist help us get our hearts ready for Christ's birth at Christmas?
6. Suggest several ways of preparing for Christmas.

FOR ME TO REMEMBER

1. Incarnation is the act of God the Son becoming Man.
2. Prophets are men who spoke in God's name.
3. To prophesy is to speak in someone else's name, especially to serve as God's voice.

FOR ME TO DO

1. Plan a moment each day to silently meditate on the second coming of Christ.
2. Compose original prayers to the Blessed Mother in preparation for Christmas.
3. Make an Advent Wreath. Any kind of Christmas wreath with four blessed candles may be used. (Do not light candles without adult supervision.)
4. Write a letter to Jesus, telling him how you are preparing for His return.

CHAPTER 14
Living With Christ During Advent

In following the liturgy of Advent, the prayers of the Church will give us much food for thought. There are many parts of the psalms used throughout the Mass that will make us think. Do you remember what psalms are? Psalms are sacred songs or poems. We can find out what they mean, discover why they are used during Advent, and what they have to do with Christ's coming to us. Finally, we can learn the special message they bring us, as we re-live the life of Christ in His Church during the season of Advent.

Do we still know the meaning of the Liturgical Year? Are we ready to begin a "new year"—that is, have we made up our minds to spend this Liturgical Year living with Christ? We know that the Church is a loving mother who wishes her children well, who wants only the best for her children. That is why the Church gives us this wonderful opportunity to do something about our lives, to make our living worthwhile, to realize the important truth that nothing really matters in this life except doing God's will. But what is God's will for us? The Advent season helps us find out.

Advent—"Coming of the Lord"

One day Christ told us exactly what God expects of us. He said: "You therefore are to be perfect, even as your heavenly Father is perfect" (Mt. 5:48). Because we are creatures we know that we cannot, of ourselves, be as perfect as God. Then why did Christ

give this command? Because He knew that there is a way of becoming like God.

The study of the Liturgical Year shows us how we can become perfect as our heavenly Father wishes. However, we must use all the means possible, natural and supernatural, especially prayer and penance, to make our hearts more worthy to receive Christ and to live His divine life. This season of Advent will teach us not only to model our lives on the life of Christ and the lives of Mary and the saints as shown in the liturgy, but to live His divine life with Him in the Church.

What is Advent? Advent is a time of preparation for the coming of Christ. People always prepare for big events. Have you ever noticed how much time is spent in preparing for a party, a banquet, a school play, or any other program? Have you ever watched the preparations for a county fair, a carnival, or a summer festival? The success of all these activities depends upon the kind of preparation that is made. How would we prepare for the president's visit if

he were to come to our city? If this is true of ordinary things and persons, how much more is it true of extraordinary things and persons. *Extraordinary* is a big word that describes something that is beyond the ordinary. What would be an extraordinary event? Our heavenly Father knew that the coming of His divine Son was an extraordinary event. He alone knew perfectly the reason for the coming of the Redeemer into the world. He showed the importance of this event by the preparation He required for the coming of Christ.

> *"When the Church celebrates the liturgy of Advent each year, she makes present this ancient expectancy of the Messiah, for by sharing in the long preparation for the Savior's first coming, the faithful renew their ardent desire for his second coming."*
>
> *—Catechism of the Catholic Church, 524*

The Jews of old prepared for the first coming of Christ. We, too, spend about four weeks in preparing ourselves for Christ's coming to us in order to be ready for His coming at the end of the world. This time of preparation is called Advent or *Coming.* How are we to prepare for Christ's coming to us? The Church suggests the very best means—prayer and penance.

We have learned that in the Mass Christ re-lives His whole life. In offering the Holy Sacrifice of the Mass with Christ we re-live Christ's life with Him. We are very closely united to Christ, and because we are one with Him we become more worthy to celebrate His coming. It is in the Mass that Christ imparts His graces to us to help us live His divine life, and to strengthen us to do whatever He requires of us. He helps us to prepare well for His coming into our hearts on Christmas Day and every day of our lives.

In order to help us in this preparation for Christ's coming, the liturgy makes each Sunday of Advent a kind of key which unlocks the mysteries of the time.

The First Sunday of Advent (Announces the Coming of Christ)

If we really want to live the life of Christ with the Church, we must first purify our hearts and minds of all that may keep Christ out of our lives. To help us get ready for Christ's coming, the Gospel for the first Sunday of Advent tells about the end of the world when Christ will come as judge of the living and the dead. Christ tells us that certain signs will announce the end of the world. Just as the new flowers on the fig tree are a sign of spring, so there will be signs before the end of the world. By reminding us of the last judgment, the Gospel makes us think about the purpose for which we were created. We know that we have been created to know, love, and serve God, and we know that Jesus came to help us. Therefore, the more closely we are united to Christ here on earth, the more easily we will obtain eternal life with God in heaven.

St. Paul tells us one way that will bring us close to Christ: "Let us," he writes, "therefore lay aside the works of darkness" (Rom. 13:12). The "works of darkness" are our sins, which alone separate us from God and keep us from living in union with Christ. The great Apostle also tells us that "it is now the hour for us to rise from sleep" (Rom. 13:11). What does St. Paul mean by *sleep?* By sleep he means spiritual laziness which keeps us from loving God with our whole hearts. This is the laziness which makes us feel satisfied with ourselves. It lets little sins become habits. This laziness can even keep us from obeying God's great commandments. How are we going to fight this evil, this spiritual laziness, during Advent?

St. Paul also warns us that "the night is far advanced; the day is at hand" (Rom. 13:12). By the word *night* the Apostle means the darkness caused by sin. The *day* is Christ Himself, who called Himself the light of the world. He comes to dwell in all men, to show them how to live. It is only through Christ that we can find our way to Him. He encourages us to practice the virtues of kindness, obedience, truthfulness, and the spirit of sacrifice. Above all, He encourages us to make and keep our hearts pure and free from sin. In this way we can obey St. Paul's warning to "lay aside the works of darkness . . . [and] put on the Lord Jesus Christ" (Rom. 13:12, 14).

St. Paul is not the only one who urges us to prepare for the coming of Christ. In his Gospel account, St. Luke takes us to the end of the world and tells us that Christ will come to judge the living and the dead. Why should the Church want us to think of death and judgment day during Advent? Are we not preparing for His coming to us on the joyful feast of Christmas? Then why should we think of such serious things as death and judgment? The Church wants us to remember Christ's last coming in order to prepare better for His coming into our hearts now. If we learn to live with Christ now, we shall be ready to meet Him as our judge.

The best way to learn how to live with Christ is to take an active part in the Mass. The Mass is the crowning act of the liturgy, and it is in the Mass that we can and should live with Christ in preparing for His coming. In the Mass Christ offers Himself to God as our Victim, and us with Him if we are willing. The different prayers of the Mass for the first Sunday of Advent encourage us to trust in God, to hope in Him, above all, to beg Him to come, for our need is very great.

During Advent it will be good for us to frequently pray: "Use Your power, Lord, we pray You, and come! With You for our protector and redeemer, may we earn deliverance and safety from the dangers that threaten us by our sins."

In this prayer our attention is drawn to the word *come.* We implore Jesus the Savior to come. Why should Jesus come to us? That we may "earn deliverance and safety from the dangers that threaten us."

It would be a good idea to learn this prayer by heart and to repeat it often as an expression of our heartfelt longing and our preparation for the coming of Christ.

The prophet Isaiah also helps us to keep in mind the main purpose of Advent, namely, the holy longing for the Savior. He has us daily repeating: "Drop down dew, ye heavens, from above, and let the clouds rain the just" (Isa. 45:8). Can you think of other ways?

The Immaculate Conception (December 8)

Perhaps the best way to prepare for Christ's coming to us is to join His own Immaculate Mother in her preparation. Mary is our model for living through, with, and in Christ. How did Mary prepare? First of all, God prepared Mary by keeping her free from the least stain of sin. In the Divine Office we read, "You are entirely beautiful, O Mary; there is no stain in you." Mary was conceived and born free from sin. That was God's part of the preparation. But what did Mary herself do to

"The Immaculate Conception shines like a beacon of light for humanity in all the ages. At the beginning of the third millennium, it guides us to believe and hope in God, in his salvation and in eternal life. In particular, it lights the way of the Church, which is committed to the new evangelization."

—Pope St. John Paul II

get ready for Jesus' coming? Like the rest of God's children, Mary had free will. Free will is God's gift to us. He wants us to use it to come closer to Him. Mary used her free will to choose only those things that would lead her to God. She chose the things that would bring her to God and make her one with Him. We should imitate her.

Baptism cleansed us from original sin, and gave us the supernatural life of grace. We became spiritually alive with grace. Often, however, we choose things that lead us away from God. Sometimes we may even choose things that kill divine life in us. We choose sin instead of Christ. When we fall by sinning, we should remember that all we have is from God and that His Son died to give us heaven. We can be helped by the example His holy Mother gave us. With her, we can strive to do all for God. We can make His wishes our wishes.

Christ is the perfect model for us. He became man to show us how to live. His mother, too, gives us the example we should follow. Like Mary, we should use our free will to choose only those things that will bring us to Christ, and make us live in and through Him. That is what Advent should mean to us. That is how we can imitate Mary in her preparation.

"He is coming!" is the constant cry of the Church during Advent. The Church wants us to get ready to receive Christ. Mary was free from sin and was beautiful because of God's grace and virtues. She was thus ready to receive Christ, the Promised One. Are we ready for His coming? "Draw us, Virgin Immaculate, and we will hurry after you." He is coming, so we must await His coming with Mary, His Mother and our Mother.

To be ready for Christ's coming, we must remember that God will be pleased with us only inasmuch as He sees Christ, His Divine Son, in us. By working with grace, by living with the Church in the mysteries of Advent, by doing our best to get rid of sin, to gain virtues, we can prepare ourselves for the coming of our loving Savior, who will give us His life and change us into Himself.

Because Mary was always united with Christ by love, she was pleasing to God. During Advent, Christ stands at the door of our hearts and knocks. He wants to come in, to make our hearts His own. But the heart that receives Him must be ready for Him. Prepare for His coming by prayer and penance. From the feast of the Immaculate Conception we can learn how to purify ourselves so that Christ will want to come to us.

Keep the following points in mind as you spend the first week of Advent with Mary:

1. Trust in God because He is so good to us.
2. Avoid sin by choosing things that please God.
3. Spend some extra time in prayer, and if possible, attend daily Mass as often as you can.
4. Imitate Christ by practicing the little virtues of obedience, kindness, purity of heart.
5. Frequently ask Jesus to come. This short prayer might help: "Come, Lord Jesus, Come!"
6. Prepare for and celebrate the feast of the Immaculate Conception in a very special manner.

The Second Sunday of Advent (Reminds Us That the Kingdom of God Is Near)

The first week of Advent told us of the coming of Christ. This week we will be told to think about the coming of God's Kingdom. The Holy Catholic Church is God's Kingdom. The words "God's Kingdom" can mean the way in which God wants to live in the members of the Church, that is, in us. The Kingdom of God means that we must make our hearts a worthy home for God. Throughout the coming week we must prepare for the Lord's visit to our hearts. In the Mass and in the Divine Office we ask God to help us get ready for the coming of His Son so that, through Him, we may serve God with pure and holy hearts.

The liturgy for this week reminds us of our longing for the coming of Christ: "Behold, the Lord will come in clouds with His full power."

St. John the Baptist

During Advent the Church calls our attention to one of God's heroes, St. John the Baptist. Jesus told us that St. John was one of the greatest persons on earth.

An angel announced the birth of St. John. Since God had a very special work for John to do, He prepared him for it. Upon Mary's greeting, John leapt in the womb of his mother, Elizabeth. Tradition holds that Jesus (who was within Mary) freed John from original sin at the moment of the Visitation. John spent his life doing penance and preaching to the people. John was very close to God and he knew he was to prepare the people for Christ. During Advent John shows us how to prepare for Christ's coming.

St. John went into the desert and there, by prayer and severe penance, prepared himself for the great work he was to do. He was the Precursor of Christ. *Precursor* is a big word, but it simply means "one who comes before" or "one who prepares the way for another." He knew that he had to prepare the hearts and minds of the people for the coming of Christ. This was very important work and John realized it. He showed that he understood what he was to do by the kind of life he led in the desert. He gave up many things to prepare himself for the great work God had given him to do.

He became a sort of spiritual giant. He was full of love for God and His honor, and he wanted only to help everyone get ready to receive Christ. By this unusual preparation John teaches us that we, too, must change our lives before Christ can come to us. Most of us are not asked to leave parents, home, and everything else as John did. The change must come in our lives. We, too, must become spiritual giants. We must bravely give up unkindness, selfishness, lying, cowardice, and other sinful habits which keep Christ out of our lives. This is one of the lessons John the Baptist teaches us.

The disciples of St. John also teach us a lesson. One day St. John, who was in prison, sent them to Christ to ask who He was. Christ answered by telling them to go back to John and tell him what they had seen: "the blind see, the lame walk, the lepers are cleansed, the deaf hear, the dead rise, the poor have the gospel preached to them" (Mt. 11:4–5). Why did Christ speak that way? To prove that He was the expected Messiah, the Redeemer who came to save the world from sin, for those were the very things the great prophets predicted Christ would do. He also wanted to impress upon the disciples that He can help us get rid of the sickness of sin.

A proverb Jesus used to teach men how to live was, "If a blind man were to guide a blind man, both would fall into a pit" (Mt. 15:14). The blindness our Lord had in mind was not that of our eyes, but of our hearts. When we refuse to help someone for Christ's sake, we are blind. We fail to see a child of God and our brother in him. We forget that Christ told us "as long as you did it for one of these, the least of my brethren, you did it for me" (Mt. 25:40).

There are also times when we are lame—we are too lazy to use our feet in doing an act of kindness, or running an errand. Can you think of other ways by which we show we are spiritually lame? Sometimes we are deaf. We don't want to hear God's voice, our conscience, warning us of danger. We don't want to hear when someone asks us for a favor. We refuse to listen when God asks us for a little sacrifice. And finally, we may even show signs of leprosy—not leprosy of the body but leprosy of the soul. If our souls are stained by sin, they can be compared to a body covered with leprosy; only Christ can cleanse us of that disease.

During Advent we should recall the words of St. Paul in his letter to the Romans. There, Paul tells us that Christ came to redeem not only the Jews but the Gentiles also. The word *Gentile* means one who does not belong to the Jewish race. The Gentiles did not know about the one true God. The knowledge of the true God was kept alive only among the Jews. St. Paul's words are: "And again Isaias says, 'There shall be the root of Jesse, and he who shall arise to rule the Gentiles . . . in him the Gentiles shall hope'" (Rom. 15:12). Christ came to be the Savior of both Jews and Gentiles.

In another place St. Paul says that we should be "of one mind towards one another according to Jesus Christ" (Rom. 15:5). He means that we must think of one another and treat one another as brothers in Christ. Does not the Lord want us to help Him come to poor pagans in far-off lands? How?

The Third Sunday of Advent (Gaudete Sunday)

The third Sunday of Advent opens the gates to an important week in the Advent Liturgy. First, we are now in the middle of the Advent season. The Feast of Christmas, when Christ the Redeemer came into this world, is almost here. Therefore, the Church prays: "The Lord is now near at hand: Come, let us adore him." During this week, too, we begin the "O Antiphons." They are parts of the Divine Office in which we earnestly beg Christ to come, not to wait any longer.

On this third Sunday of Advent the Church calls upon us to rejoice. "Rejoice in the Lord always: again, I say, rejoice . . . for the Lord is near." The Church wishes us to be happy at the thought of Christ's coming for which Advent prepares us. Christ is longing to come into our hearts and make them alive with His life. Do we long to receive Him? Now that we understand better the meaning of the Mass, we can unite ourselves with the priest in offering Christ and ourselves with Him to the eternal Father.

In the Gospel readings during Advent, St. John the Baptist continues to be our helper. He tells us some of the things we ought to do to prepare well for Christ's coming to us. We all like to tell people who we are and what we are. We want them to think well of us, to think we are someone important. Again St. John proves that he is different. Priests and Levites ask who he is. The first thing he tells them is who he is not. This shows that St. John was really a great man. He boldly tells that he is not Elijah; he is not a prophet; he is only "the voice of one crying in the desert" (Jn. 1:23). What does he mean by calling himself a voice? Whose voice was he?

The Gospel, which tells us so much about St. John the Baptist, directs our thoughts to prayer and penance. That is what John meant by the words: "Make straight the way of the Lord" (Jn. 1:23). He is talking about Christ's coming and how necessary it is for us to remove everything that will keep Christ from coming to us. We know very well what keeps Christ from ruling over us. Sin is the only roadblock in the "path of the Lord."

By prayer and penance and by receiving the sacraments frequently we can cleanse ourselves of everything that will prevent

Christ's union with us. If we want Christ to live and act through us, we must imitate St. John the Baptist, who teaches us what to do to please God.

What would you say if Christ were to ask you, "Who are you?" Your answer would prove what you think of Christ and what you know about Christ. Are you wondering why? As members of the Mystical Body of Christ, we should be living the life of Christ with Him in the Church. We have this great chance to live with Christ in the Holy Sacrifice of the Mass each day and to re-live the drama of His life during the Church Year. Are we living the life of Christ? Are we preparing for His coming by imitating the example of St. John the Baptist? If so, Christ will joyfully come to us to make us one with Him. When men see us acting with the charity, the justice, the kindness, the courage, and the patience of Christ they will know that we have "put on Christ."

Ember Days

We learned earlier in the year that the prayer of the Church is usually one of praise, thanksgiving, and adoration. The Church also urges her faithful children to beg from God the things they need. The Mass is one of the best ways not only of praising and giving glory to God, but also of asking Him for blessings and of begging His pardon for sin. In the extraordinary form, the Church has set aside special days of prayer and penance at the beginning of each of the four seasons of the year: winter, spring, summer, and autumn. They are known as Ember Days, and fall on the Wednesday, Friday, and Saturday of the Ember weeks.

During these days we pray for the graces and blessings we need and to do penance for our past sins. We need these days of extra fervent prayer and sacrifice to strengthen our life of union with God and to thank God for His many gifts of nature and grace. We must

> *"And Mary rising up in those days, went into the hill country with haste into a city of Juda. And she entered into the house of Zachary, and saluted Elizabeth."*
>
> *—Luke 1:39–40*

do penance for our own sins and for the sins of the whole world.

Finally, we pray especially for priests so that God will bless them and give them the grace and the strength to do the great work for which they were chosen. We should also pray that many more young men will listen to God calling them to serve Him in the priesthood and so continue the work which Jesus Christ, the great High Priest, began while living in this world.

Ember Wednesday and Friday of this season are devoted to the Immaculate Mother of God.

The Gospel of the Mass on Ember Wednesday tells the story of the annunciation, when Mary became the Mother of God. The antiphons in the Divine Office re-emphasize the annunciation, and make it clear that our minds should be occupied with the message during the entire day ". . . the angel Gabriel was sent . . . to a virgin betrothed to a man named Joseph . . . and the virgin's name was Mary" (Lk. 1:26–27). "Behold the handmaid of the Lord; be it done to me according to thy word" (Lk. 1:38).

The emphasis in the liturgy on Ember Friday is placed on

the beautiful story of the visitation of the Blessed Virgin Mary. Having received Christ she turns to do an act of kindness. We see her hurry through the Judean hills to visit Elizabeth. We hear the great song of thanksgiving—the Magnificat. "My soul magnifies the Lord: and my spirit rejoices in God my Saviour" (Lk. 1:46). Mary thanks God for choosing her to become the Mother of Christ. She also expresses her deep appreciation for God's great gift to man, a Saviour. Often repeat this prayer of our Lady to thank God for His numerous graces.

In the Mass prayers for Ember Saturday we recall how Christ came as God-Man to save us from sin, how He comes to live in us now, and how He will come as judge at the end of the world. These prayers refer to light and darkness. Christ, the Light of the world, comes to drive away the darkness of sin and death.

The Divine Office for Ember Saturday is rich with holy thoughts of the coming of Jesus Christ. In the morning it recalls the annunciation scene and Mary's consent to become the Mother of God. Other prayers, such as the following, bring to mind the nearness of Christmas and give us much food for meditation and prayer.

"Sound the trumpet in Sion the day of the Lord is coming so soon: behold, he will come to deliver us, alleluia, alleluia."

"Come, O Lord, and do not linger on the way."

"The Lord is coming; go out to meet him, saying: Great is his beginning, and of his reign there will be no end."

The Fourth Sunday of Advent (Tells Us That Christ's Coming Is Near)

The liturgy for the fourth Sunday of Advent makes Christ very real to us: it tells that His coming is very near. St. John the Baptist continues his warning to do penance: "Make ready the way of the Lord, make straight his paths. Every valley shall be filled, and every mountain and hill shall be brought low, and the crooked shall be made straight, and the rough ways smooth; and all mankind shall see the salvation of God" (Lk. 3:4–6).

In the prayers of the Mass for this Sunday we beg Christ to come and help us to use all the graces He gives us as medicine against the poison of sin. Let us recall the words of St. John the

Baptist which are so fitting as a meditation during this last week of Advent. First, St. John the Baptist tells us that "every valley shall be filled." What does John mean by the valley? He means the things that are lacking in our spiritual life. Until now we have tried to get rid of sin because sin keeps Christ out of our lives. Now we must take the valley of our life and fill it with the virtues that make us pleasing to God. Christ will be very happy to find in our hearts the virtues of cheerful obedience, reverence, courage, love, kindness, purity, thoughtfulness, and unselfishness.

The second warning of St. John the Baptist, "Every mountain and hill shall be brought low," or made level, clearly shows us that we must put Christ first in everything we do. We must overcome pride, selfishness, and everything that seems to make us think or feel that we are better than others. What are the little hills in our lives? They may be bad habits or venial sins. These little hills lessen our love of Jesus and are, therefore, displeasing to Him. Finally the big mountain of "self" may really keep Christ out altogether. This is the most important part of the preparation—self must give way to Christ. It must take second or last place. St. John did this in his life. He wanted Christ to increase—that is, to grow, to be known and loved by others—and he himself wanted to be forgotten altogether.

St. John wants us to be ready for Christ. His next warning is, "the crooked [ways] shall be made straight." What are the crooked ways in our lives? When Christ comes, He wants all of us, our whole being. He does not want any little dark corners where the enemy, the devil, is still at home. Perhaps we can straighten out the crooked ways of carelessness about little sins, of playing with temptations, of little habits of lying or stealing, of laziness when it comes to prayer. Perhaps there are other areas of sin we can make straight with Christ's help.

In a final warning John tells us that "the rough ways [shall be made] smooth." How carefully John wants us to prepare! He is concerned about the roughness in our characters. Since he wants us to show Christ to others, he asks us to polish up what is not Christlike in our characters. To remove this roughness, we must watch our tempers, be calm and quiet when someone gives us trouble, be courteous and gentle, and kind and forgiving when someone has hurt us. Following these suggestions, we shall do what St. Paul tells us to do—"put on the Lord Jesus Christ." Then our heavenly Father will surely recognize His divine Son in us.

In our prayer during this last week of Advent, let us think of Mary who was so closely united to Christ during this time of waiting. She teaches us by her example how closely we should be united to Christ when He comes to us in Holy Communion. Mary was the living tabernacle in whom Christ lived for nine months before He was born. We, too, become living tabernacles when Christ comes to us.

> *"The crooked [ways] shall be made straight."*

The Divine Office echoes our holy and strong desire for the Redeemer. "Sound the trumpet in Sion, the day of the Lord is coming." Who is this Lord we are awaiting? "Behold, the Desired of all nations shall come, and the house of the Lord shall be filled with glory, alleluia." What will happen when the Lord comes? "The crooked shall be made straight, and the rough ways smooth: come, Lord, do not linger on the way, alleluia."

Not many days remain until Christmas. Although the whole Advent season has been a time of special preparation, let us now make sure that we are ready for the arrival of the King. Just as we clean the house before someone special comes, so now we should cleanse ourselves by receiving the sacraments. Then with the Church we can repeat joyously: "God shall come from Lebanon, and the brightness that is his shall be like light itself." "I will look toward the Lord, I will wait for God my Savior."

The Seven Great Antiphons (December 17–23)

As the time of waiting and preparing is drawing to a close, the Church can hardly wait for the coming of Christ. Again and again she earnestly begs Him to come, not to wait any longer, but come. She makes use of some very old parts of the Divine Office when she pleads with the Savior to come. These parts of the Divine Office are the Seven Great Antiphons, or the "O Antiphons".

The Seven Great Antiphons

O Sapientia:	O Wisdom . . .
O Adonai:	O Leader . . .
O Radix Jesse:	O Root of Jesse . . .
O Clavis David:	O Key of David . . .
O Oriens:	O Orient . . .
O Rex Gentium:	O King of Gentiles . . .
O Emmanuel:	O God With Us . . .

Ero Cras: I Will Be Tomorrow

When arranged from bottom to top, the first initials of the Antiphons spell the Latin words *ero cras* meaning "I will be tomorrow" or "I will come tomorrow."

The subject of these prayers is the majesty of the Savior, His wisdom, His holiness, His power and love as King and Redeemer of the world, and His interest in each man that He has created. They show our great yearning for Christ, our Redeemer.

December 17

"O Wisdom, who comest out of the mouth of the Most High, reaching from end to end, and ordering all things mightily and sweetly: come and teach us the way of prudence."

In this antiphon we ask the Son of God, the Wisdom proceeding from the Eternal Father, to come and teach us the way in which we should walk.

December 18

"O Leader of the house of Israel, who didst appear to Moses in the burning bush, and didst give him the law on Sinai: come and redeem us with thine outstretched arm."

Here we show that we recognize the Majesty of God. The verse is a prayer to the Lord of lords of a new kingdom whose citizens are redeemed from sin and are in need of infinite mercy. We cry: Come and redeem us!

December 19

"O Root of Jesse, who standest for an ensign of the people, before whom kings shall keep silence, and to whom the Gentiles shall pray: come to deliver us and tarry now no more."

Christ came from the root, that is the family, of Jesse. He was born in poor surroundings to prove that riches and pomp are not necessary for a king. We are reminded that Christ is near, and ask Him to deliver us from all evil and not to wait longer.

December 20

"O Key of David, and Scepter of the house of Israel, who openest and no man shutteth; who shuttest and no man openeth; come and lead the captive from the prison-house, him that sitteth in darkness and in the shadow of death."

David is a figure of Christ who is to come and open the gates of heaven.

December 21

"O Oriens (i.e., rising sun), brightness of eternal life, and Sun of Justice: come and enlighten them that sit in darkness and in the shadow of death."

Here we call Christ the Day Star, the Sun of Justice, for the darkness is being scattered and Christ, the Light, begins to rise. In this light we see ourselves better and realize how precious we are in the sight of God. With Mary and Joseph we unite and wait for Christ the Light of the World.

December 22

"O King of Gentiles and their Desire, thou cornerstone that makest both one: come and deliver man whom thou didst form out of the dust of the earth."

This antiphon is sinful mankind's plea to be redeemed. We must share with Christ His great desire to save souls. Prayer and sacrifice will obtain grace for sinners.

December 23

"O God With Us (Emmanuel), our King and Lawgiver, the Expectation of the Nations, and their Savior: come and save us, O Lord, our God."

On the final day before the vigil of Christmas we greet Christ as our Emmanuel, that is God With Us. We make an act of adoration and petition at the throne of God. Our prayer begins with

Emmanuel, God With Us, because Jesus, our Savior and our God, has come to save us. We ask Him to come to be our King and Lawgiver, and promise Him obedience and loyalty.

FOR ME TO REVIEW

Questions

1. What does "Advent" mean?
2. How long does it last?
3. What is the real purpose of Advent?
4. Explain the words of St. Paul, "it is now the hour for us to rise from sleep."
5. Why is it fitting that the feast of the Immaculate Conception should come in Advent?
6. How can Mary help us to prepare for the coming of Christ?
7. What great work did St. John the Baptist have to do?
8. Why does St. Paul tell us we should treat one another as brothers and sisters?
9. Why does the Church want us to rejoice on the third Sunday of Advent?
10. How should we prepare for Christ's coming to us?
11. Explain the following gospel texts:

    "Every valley shall be filled."
    "Every mountain and hill shall be made level."
    "The crooked ways shall be made straight."
    "The rough ways shall be made smooth."

12. What are the Seven Great Antiphons? What do they mean?

FOR ME TO REMEMBER

1. Advent means "coming."
2. Advent is a time of preparation for the coming of Christ.
3. God the Father prepared the whole human race for the coming of His divine Son.
4. Living the life of Christ in the Church, by means of the Mass, is the most essential way of preparing for Christ's coming.
5. Mary helps us prepare for the coming of Christ.
6. Mary was preserved from all sin, original and actual.
7. Sin alone keeps Christ from us.
8. St. John the Baptist is the Forerunner of Christ.
9. St. John prepared for his great work by prayer and penance.
10. We also must prepare for Christ's coming by prayer and penance.
11. Christ came to save all people.
12. During the third week of Advent the Church wants us to rejoice because Christ is near.
13. As members of Christ's Mystical Body, we must live the life of Christ and show Christ to others.
14. The great "O Antiphons" are very old parts of the Divine Office. They are used to beg Christ to hurry and come to be our Savior.

FOR ME TO DO

1. Make a list of the things you can do to help you live for Christ during Advent.
2. Tell in a few words how St. John the Baptist imitated Christ. Tell how you can imitate St. John in preparing for Christ's coming.
3. Illustrate each of the seven Antiphons and explain their meaning.
4. Read the life of St. John the Baptist. Dramatize the meeting between Jesus and St. John.
5. Learn and memorize the following hymn: O Come, O Come, Emmanuel.
6. On the Feast of the Immaculate Conception arrange a *Mary Candle*. With the help of an adult, use a big white candle arising from a white rose to symbolize the purity of the Virgin Mother. Place it next to an empty crib or before a statue of our Lady. Keep it unlit until Christmas Eve. On Christmas Eve, light the candle. The flame signifies that Christ, the Light of the World, has come through the Virgin Mother.

CHAPTER 15

Living With Christ at Christmas

In this chapter we shall learn the real meaning of Christmas as the Church teaches it to us in the liturgy. We shall learn it in a way in which we can hope to get the true spirit of this joyful season. It is a spirit of joy because this season recalls the birth of our Savior. It is a spirit of thanks for God's goodness to us. It is a spirit of love and respect for our Lady, who was made the Mother of God. We shall follow the liturgy on Christmas Day so that we can understand and do our part well in the celebration. In this way we can share in the happiness of the Church and be more pleasing to the Infant Savior in the manger.

The Vigil of Christmas

The best way to prepare for Christmas is to serve God faithfully every day. And to prepare to celebrate Christ's birth worthily, the finest means is to join in the liturgy of Christ's Church. The Mass on the day before Christmas, or the *vigil,* is filled with joyful prayers to tell us how very close Christ is, and in the extraordinary form, the priest wears the violet vestments of penance. The Church thanks God for the joy He puts into our hearts by sending His Son to us as Redeemer, and we pray that God may make us ready for Christ when He returns in glory to judge men at the end of the world.

At the beginning of the Mass the Church reminds us that the Lord shall come, and that tomorrow we shall see His glory. What

does this mean? It means first that we should get ready to greet the Babe of Bethlehem, and that we must always keep ourselves ready to see Christ as our Judge when we die.

All day long during the vigil the Church keeps repeating in the Divine Office the key message: *Christ is coming!*

"This day you shall know that the Lord is coming, and tomorrow you shall see His glory.

"Sanctify yourselves, O children of Israel, says the Lord, for tomorrow the Lord will come down and remove all sickness from you.

"Tomorrow the iniquity of the earth will be blotted out; and the Savior of the world will rule over us."

Christmas in Bethlehem

On Christmas Day the Church cries out in joy: "Christ is born to us: Come, let us adore!" and she sings the beautiful hymn: "Jesus Redeemer of all men!"

Imagine that you are in the Holy Land when Christ was born in the little town of Bethlehem. Think of the many things that happened at His coming.

Recall first how the Archangel Gabriel told Mary the good news that God was to become her Son, and how she agreed to become His Mother. Filled with happiness and joy, Mary hurried to Judea, to St. Elizabeth, her cousin. It was during her visit there that St. John the Baptist was especially blessed by God and chosen to prepare the people for Christ's coming. Later there was the tiresome journey of Mary and Joseph to Bethlehem, to give their names for the census. Mary was about to give birth to her divine Son, yet she and Joseph could find only a cave as their shelter. That night the angels announced the glad tidings of Christ's birth to the humble shepherds in the fields. These poor men hurried to welcome Christ into the world.

Christmas in the Church

On the great feast of the birth of our Lord and Savior, Jesus Christ, the Church expresses her joy by celebrating three Masses. Her prayers and songs are full of joy! The vestments are white, the color of joy! The white tells of the glory of the divinity, the beauty of the Savior who was born in Bethlehem, and the purity of His Virgin-Mother. It reminds us of the pure hearts we should have when we come to visit His crib.

In the extraordinary form, there are three different Masses celebrated on Christmas Day. Each of the three Masses for Christmas has beautiful prayers. By following these prayers and thinking about them we will be better able to think and do the things Christ wishes us to.

The *First Mass on Christmas* is celebrated at midnight. It is called the Angels' Mass. Its Gospel tells the story of the birth of Christ in the stable at Bethlehem. No one except Mary and Joseph knows the mystery. Then the angel announces the glad news to the shepherds. ". . . behold, I bring you good news of great joy which

shall be to all the people; for there has been born to you today in the town of David a Savior, who is Christ the Lord" (Lk. 2:10–12).

The Redeemer has come and has taught us how to live. He will come again, to judge us and to lead us to His Father. Are we ready? By receiving Christ in Holy Communion, we can learn from Him how to get ready. As we would have wanted to go to the Babe of Bethlehem on the first Christmas night, so now we will want to approach Him in Holy Communion.

In the *Second Mass at Daybreak,* or the Shepherds' Mass, we join the shepherds as they hurry to the Infant Jesus to adore, praise, and thank Him for coming down to earth. He came in the darkness of night, but He is the divine light which sends away the darkness of sin.

All during Advent we have prayed for Christ the King to come. Now in the prayers of this Mass, the Church says: "Behold thy King comes, holy, the Savior of the world." He comes to us in a royal way, in a way in which only a king can come. When we freely give ourselves to God, we are sure of true peace and happiness. In the *Third Mass,* which is celebrated during the day, St. John's Gospel reminds us that Christ as God has lived from all eternity in heaven, with God the Father and God the Holy Spirit. In the other two Masses we prayed with the angels and the shepherds. In this Mass we join with the whole Christian world in recognizing the Christ Child as our King, our Redeemer, and our God. In the Gospel, too, St. John reminds the people who believe in God and who love God that they will become "sons of God" for they are born "of God." But he also reminds us that He "came unto his own, and his own received him not." Are we "his own"? Do some of us refuse to accept Him?

When we assist at Mass and receive Holy Communion on Christmas Day we are very closely united with our Savior. We can think of ourselves as being like the city of Bethlehem. The flickering candles on the altar are the stars. And our hearts are the manger. All these happy thoughts we can express in the hymn of the angels on the first Christmas night, "Glory to God in the highest, and peace on earth among men of good will" (Lk. 2:14).

> *"Only when Christ is formed in us will the mystery of Christmas be fulfilled in us."*
>
> *—Catechism of the Catholic Church, 526*

Christmas in Our Hearts

On Christmas Day the Church sings: "This day Christ was born; this day the Savior appeared; this day the Angels sing on earth, and the Archangels rejoice; Glory to God in the highest."

Try to enter into the spirit of the Church. Make some return to God our Savior who became so little and humble to save us. Give back to Him a little of the love that He gave us. Never forget who He is and what we are! He is worthy of our deepest love and adoration.

We have learned how our Blessed Mother prepared for the coming of her divine Son. She can teach us to be kind and loving to our neighbors and playmates, to be willing to do hard things for God, to be respectful to our parents and to those in charge of us, and to be humble at all times. She remembered how great God is and so was careful to obey His wishes. Do we obey God's wishes at all times? Do we keep His commandments? Mary was sinless and pure of heart. Do we avoid all pictures, places, and persons that can lead us to evil? Her love for Him was as great as only the love of God's mother can be. Do we love God above all things? Above all persons? Are we willing to fight temptation and do what is right to prove our love for God? Our Blessed Mother's Christmas was truly in her heart!

Like Christ, we must make God's will our will. We must do things in ways that please God. Then we can be sure of a true Christmas in our hearts.

FOR ME TO REVIEW

Catechism Lesson

75. **Q. On what day was Christ born?**
A. Christ was born on Christmas day in a stable at Bethlehem, over two thousand years ago.

Questions

1. Use each group of words in one complete, correct statement.
   A. prepare—Catholic Church—liturgy
   B. joyful—vigil—Mass prayers
   C. joy—expectation—vigil
2. Which statements are true?
   A. According to the liturgy of the Church, Christmas time lasts about ten days.
   B. Before the Archangel Gabriel came to Mary she knew that she would be the Mother of the Savior.
   C. Christmas really means Christ coming into our hearts and lives.
3. What things did Mary do to have a happy Christmas?
4. How can you have a Christmas like Mary's?
5. Complete the following statements:
   A. The Christmas Midnight Mass is called . . . .
   B. We call the Mass at Dawn . . . .
   C. In the Third Mass, the Gospel reminds us that Christ is . . . .

FOR ME TO REMEMBER

1. On the vigil of Christmas the Mass prayers tell of the great joy and expectation of Christmas Day as if it were already here.
2. In the Liturgical Year, Christmas time begins with the first

Sunday of Advent and lasts until the Baptism of our Lord (or in the calendar of the extraordinary form, until Septuagesima Sunday).

3. The *Midnight Mass* is called the Angels' Mass. It tells of the birth of our Savior in Bethlehem and of His birth in our hearts through grace.
4. The *Mass at Dawn* is called the Shepherds' Mass. We join the shepherds as they come to adore their Savior and their King.
5. In the *Third Mass* the prayers tell us of our Savior's eternal life in heaven with God the Father and God the Holy Spirit.

FOR ME TO DO

1. Explain the word *vigil* and tell why it helps us celebrate a holy day, especially Christmas.
2. Make a few original prayers telling the Christ Child how each year you understand better the meaning of His birthday.
4. Explain the meaning of the three Masses on Christmas Day.
5. Receive Holy Communion during the Sacrifice of the Mass. Thank the Infant Child for the great privilege you have of holding Him in your heart. Ask Him to make you strong to fight temptation, strong to do what is right. Ask Him to help you act like Him.
6. Imagine you are a little shepherd visiting Jesus in the cave. Write a short paragraph telling how you feel kneeling in the presence of Jesus, Mary, and Joseph.
7. Redecorate your Advent wreath with bright ribbons and ornaments and use it as a door or window decoration or a centerpiece on your dining room table.

CHAPTER 16
Living With Christ During the Christmas Season

How happy we always are to celebrate the glorious feast of Christmas, the birthday of the Christ Child! With all the other members of God's family, we prepare our hearts by prayer and penance during the long season of Advent. Finally, the day arrives, and with the Church we welcome the newborn Babe into our hearts. But one day is not enough for our joy; so the Church continues the celebration for several weeks. Holy Mother Church, through her sacred liturgy, wants us to grow in divine life by celebrating with her.

The feast of the Christ Child's birth proved to us how much God loved us. He loved us so much that He sent His only-begotten Son to live among us. Christ, eternal Love, came to take our sins upon Himself.

The three feasts immediately following Christmas Day show us what a Christ-life means. These are the feasts of St. Stephen the first martyr, St. John the virgin apostle, and the tiny victims of Herod's jealousy, the Holy Innocents. They show us how we must serve Christ in courage, in purity, in communal love and innocence. The feasts also remind us that the joy and happiness of Christmas are only a beginning of the joy and happiness we shall enjoy united with God in heaven.

St. Stephen, the First Martyr (December 26)

St. Stephen was one of the seven deacons or helpers of the Apostles. He led a Christlike life. He shows us that living with Christ means serving others for Christ as well as suffering for Christ. St. Stephen cared for the poor and needy: he taught, he preached, he baptized.

Because he was not afraid to preach about Christ, St. Stephen made many enemies. He was brought before the Jewish council where false witnesses accused him of blasphemy, that is, insulting God.

During his trial St. Stephen, filled with the Holy Spirit, looked up to heaven. He began to speak words of divine wisdom. This is what he told the people: "Behold, I see the heavens opened, and the Son of Man standing at the right hand of God" (Acts 7:56). St. Stephen's faith in God remained firm, unshaken. He spoke fearlessly of the divinity of Christ! Are we as brave? Is our faith that strong?

The enemies of St. Stephen became so angry that they took him out of the city and stoned him to death. Like Christ, his Master, Stephen's last words were words of forgiveness. As the shower of stones fell about him he prayed: "Lord, do not lay this sin against them" (Acts 7:60). Thus, St. Stephen, the first martyr, gave the gift of his life to the newborn Babe of Bethlehem.

"Behold, I see the heavens opened, and the Son of Man standing at the right hand of God" (Acts 7:56).

By giving his life for his faith St. Stephen showed us what being one with Christ means. By asking God to forgive those who were stoning him to death, St. Stephen showed us how Christ wants us to love our neighbor. We may not be called, as St. Stephen was, to shed our blood for Christ; but there may be many times when we will be asked to profess our faith in Christ's teachings.

As children of Christ's Mystical Body, we should remain near the crib of the Infant Savior and learn the lessons of faith and love St. Stephen learned so well. Then we should try to live for Christ and with Christ as he did. If we do, Christ will live in us and help us bear our sufferings, and many will join His Church.

St. John, Apostle and Evangelist (December 27)

The second feast after Christmas is that of St. John, the beloved Apostle. It is from St. John's Gospel that we have learned so much about the divinity of Christ. Divinity means that Christ was God.

St. John is often called the Apostle of Love. His long life was a life of love: love of his divine Master and love of his neighbor. He imitated Christ especially in his love of purity and modesty. How Christ must have loved St. John is told by the Apostle himself. He tells us that at the Last Supper "one of his disciples, he whom

Jesus loved, was reclining at Jesus' bosom" (Jn. 13:23). It was to the care of this loving disciple that Christ, when dying on the cross, entrusted His Mother Mary. We, too, must learn to love Christ so much that He will give His Mother to us, also.

As we kneel at the crib of the Christ Child during this Christmas time St. John's lesson of love, preached to the early Christians, reminds us of the greatness of God's love for us in sending to earth His divine Son for our redemption. Let us show God that we appreciate His love for us by our imitation of the courage, the purity, and the charity of St. John the Apostle.

The Holy Innocents (December 28)

On the third day after Christ's birth we celebrate the feast of the Holy Innocents. How much do you remember about them from the Bible story?

King Herod waited anxiously for the return of the Wise Men so that he would know where the newborn King was to be found. When they did not return, Herod became very angry. In order to be rid of the new King, Herod sent his soldiers to destroy all the baby boys under two years of age who were in Bethlehem or in the surrounding neighborhood. The soldiers snatched the babies from the arms of their mothers and killed them. How the mothers of these innocent babies mourned and wept for them! However, the baby Jesus was not harmed. An angel had warned St. Joseph to take Jesus and Mary to Egypt to escape Herod.

Long, long before the birth of Christ the prophet Jeremiah foretold the death of these children and the grief of their mothers. St. Matthew's Gospel quotes the prophecy:

> *"A voice was heard in Rama, weeping and loud lamentation; Rachel weeping for her children, and she would not be comforted, because they are no more."*
>
> *—Mt. 2:18*

On this day the Church mourns with the mothers of Bethlehem. She changes her white vestments of Christmas joy to red (like the blood of Martyrs), and omits the Gloria and the Alleluias from the Mass. In today's Mass we pray with the Church: "O God, whose praise the martyred Innocents confessed this day, not in speech, but by death: mortify within us all vices: that Thy faith which our tongues profess, our lives by their actions may confess." Living with Christ in joy, we are never far from the thought of Penance.

Like the Holy Innocents, we should show by our actions that we, too, would give up our lives rather than deny Christ. From them we should learn that at times God permits even the innocent to suffer.

Feast of the Holy Family

(The Sunday after Christmas for the ordinary form, or the Sunday after Epiphany for the extraordinary form.)

A very lovely and most appropriate feast of the Christmas season is the feast of the Holy Family. On the feast of the Holy Family we find Jesus, Mary, and Joseph giving us the perfect example of how to live as a family. In the Mass for this feast, we ask Christ to bless our homes and our families that they, too, may be holy.

In the Mass prayer we are told to rejoice with Mary and Joseph because they were chosen by God to be the mother and foster father of His divine Son, Jesus.

Ask Jesus for the grace to imitate the virtues of the Holy Family so that we may share their joys in Heaven. What are some of the virtues which are so necessary to make our family life pleasing to God? By practicing love, obedience, humility, patience, forgiveness, and helpfulness as they were practiced by Jesus, Mary and Joseph, we will please God.

"For every believer, and especially for Christian families, the humble dwelling place in Nazareth is an authentic school of the Gospel. Here we admire, put into practice, the divine plan to make the family an intimate community of life and love; here we learn that every Christian family is called to be a small "domestic church" that must shine with the Gospel virtues. Recollection and prayer, mutual understanding and respect, personal discipline and community asceticism and a spirit of sacrifice, work and solidarity are typical features that make the family of Nazareth a model for every home."

POPE ST. JOHN PAUL II

Our Lady and the saints ask all of us to pray the rosary, especially as a family. The Virgin Mother's plea for saying the family rosary was meant to teach us that the secret of peace in family life lies in imitating the virtues of the Holy Family. Do you think that the Holy Family prayed often? How often?

From the Gospel of the Feast of the Holy Family we learn about Christ's perfect obedience to Mary and Joseph. We have often heard the story of how Jesus was lost and after three days was found in the temple. Although He explained to Mary and Joseph that He must be about His Father's business, the Gospel says, "And he went down with them and came to Nazareth, and was subject to them" (Lk. 2:51).

We can try to be perfectly obedient as Jesus was. We should ask our divine Model to help us to grow each day in wisdom and in grace.

Solemnity of Mary, the Holy Mother of God; Octave of the Nativity (New Year's Day—January 1)

January first, as you know, is the first day of an ordinary year. It is also an important day in the Church for two major reasons. It is the Octave of the Nativity, that is, the eighth day after Christmas, and a holy day of obligation. It was on this day that our Lord was circumcised. In the ordinary form, it is also the day that has been chosen to commemorate Mary, the Mother of God. After all, it is Mary who is the "Bearer of God" and the one who will—along with Joseph—faithfully take Jesus to be circumcised on the eighth day of his life.

Circumcision was a ceremony required by the Old Law. According to this law every baby boy was circumcised when he was eight days old. In keeping with the law, the Christ Child was circumcised and shed His blood for the first time. Jesus was not bound by the law because He was God, but He kept it because that was the will of His Father. What a lesson of perfect obedience we can learn from the Christ Child! Do we try to keep His laws, the commandments, the way He kept the Jewish laws?

On this day Christ, as a tiny child, begins His life of suffering. Remember that He came to earth to suffer and die for us because of His great love for each one of us. Do we imitate the Christ Child when we have little sufferings and pains? Do we fret and fuss, or do we try to suffer with patience and make our sufferings pleasing to God?

This day reminds us that Christ allowed His own flesh to be cut and His blood to flow. Is Christ trying to tell us how we must live if we would live with Him? Even as a baby He shows us how to suffer.

Feast of the Epiphany
(January 6)

On the night that Jesus was born, the angels announced to the shepherds, who represented the Jews, the chosen people of the Old Testament, that the Messiah had come and that God had become man. This wonderful news was also given to the Gentile nations. God made it known to the Wise Men from the East who came to Bethlehem. We celebrate this on the Epiphany.

The feast of the Epiphany is one of the oldest and greatest in the Church Year. *Epiphany* means "a showing." On this day Jesus showed Himself to the Wise Men and to the whole world.

On the feast of the Epiphany the Church celebrates three important mysteries in the life of Christ. In these mysteries Christ reveals Himself as being truly God and truly Man. These mysteries are the coming of the Magi; the Miracle at Cana; and Christ's Baptism in the Jordan.

Today, in the Vespers, which is the evening prayer of the Church, we are reminded of these three mysteries: "We celebrate a festival adorned by three miracles: this day, a star led the Magi to the manger; this day, water was changed into wine at the marriage-feast; this day, Christ willed to be baptized in the Jordan for our salvation."

The Adoration of the Magi

In the first mystery we learn of the Wise Men, or Magi, as they are sometimes called. They were led by a star to the newborn King of the Jews. Remember how they traveled to Jerusalem and came to King Herod to ask where the new King would be found? They were told to go to Bethlehem. As soon as they left Jerusalem the star appeared again, to lead them to Bethlehem, where Christ was born. "And entering the house, they found the child with Mary his mother, and falling down they worshipped him" (Mt. 2:11).

Why did these Magi, who were pagans, worship the Christ Child? God had told them about the birth of His Son, and had led them to Bethlehem by the star.

The Wise Men offered Christ Jesus gifts of gold, frankincense, and myrrh. Gold is a gift for kings. Christ is the King of heaven and earth. Frankincense, a symbol of prayer, is a gift to be offered to God alone. Christ is God. The gift of myrrh, which was used for death and burial, was given to

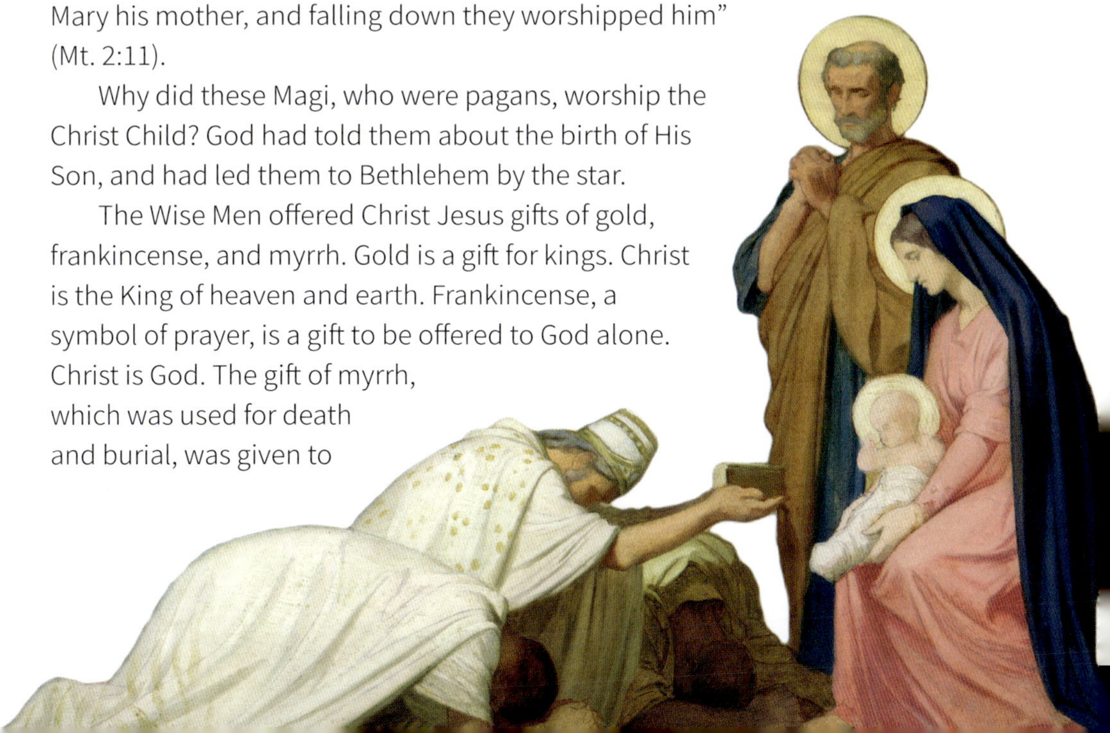

the Christ Child because He was also Man, who would suffer and die and be buried.

Like the Wise Men who brought their gifts to the Christ Child, we should bring our gifts—the gold of charity, the sweet smelling incense of prayer, and the myrrh of suffering and penance.

The Miracle at Cana

The next mystery which the feast of the Epiphany recalls is the miracle at Cana.

The marriage feast had been prepared, and the Mother of Jesus was present. During the feast all the wine was used. Mary felt sorry for the people. She told her Son, "They have no wine." As Mary told Jesus of the needs of these people, she also tells Him of our needs.

When Jesus answered His Mother, "My hour is not yet come," He meant that He would perform this miracle not as Mary's son, but as the Son of God. Mary understood her Son and told the waiters to do whatever Jesus should say. Jesus commanded that the waterpots be filled with water, and then said, "Draw out now." The waterpots no longer held water, but the very best wine.

By this miracle Jesus showed Himself to be God, and His disciples believed in Him. The miracle is full of wonderful lessons and thoughts.

In our daily lives we can show Christ to others. We can show that He lives within us if we act as He acts. When we receive Christ in Holy Communion He gives us His divine life and strength so that we may become more Christlike in all our actions. Do our neighbors see and sense the fact that Christ lives and acts through us? If we are really living with Christ, they do. This miracle also reveals how our Blessed Mother anticipates her children's needs and intercedes for them.

Christ's Baptism in the Jordan

The third mystery which is celebrated on the feast of the Epiphany is Christ's baptism in the Jordan, at the start of His public life.

When Jesus was being baptized, St. John saw the heavens open and the Spirit of God, the Holy Spirit, come down as a Dove upon Christ. He heard the voice of God the Father saying: "This is my beloved Son, in whom I am well pleased." Here, God the Father and God the Holy Spirit made known to St. John the Baptist, and to us as well, that Christ is the Son of God. Thank God for showing us that Christ is His divine Son. Thank Him for having given us the waters of Baptism to cleanse us from our sins and make us, His adopted children; brothers of Christ.

The Baptism of Our Lord

The feast of the Baptism of our Lord marks the last day of the Christmas Season in the ordinary form liturgical calendar. "Behold the lamb of God" (Jn. 1:29) were the words John the Baptist spoke when he saw Christ coming toward him. He wanted to let his followers know that the promised Redeemer was now in their midst. John's work of preparing a way for the Lord could now come to an end, for the Lord had come and was ready to begin His work of redemption.

Jesus is still with us. John's baptism was not a sacrament, but Jesus allowed John to baptize Him in order to show us that we would need the sacrament of Baptism. In Baptism we "put on Christ," and become living members of His Mystical Body. Jesus showed Himself to John and his followers in the flesh; He wants to show Himself to the people of our day by living in us.

The Presentation of Our Lord, or the Purification of Mary (February 2)

February second, the fortieth day after Christmas, is the Feast of the Presentation of our Lord (ordinary form). In the extraordinary form, this feast is referred to as the Purification of Our Lady.

Joseph and Mary, in obedience to the Law of Moses, carried the Child from Bethlehem and presented Him to God in the temple and then offered the necessary sacrifice. He was bought back for five shekels (about $6), according to the law for a first-born boy.

These two happenings tell us that the feast is twofold—it is a feast of our Lord and also of our Lady. Jesus, the Son of God, did not have to obey the Law of Moses; however, He wanted to give us an example of obedience and humility. How does our obedience compare with His?

After the ceremony in the temple, an aged and holy man named Simeon met Mary, Joseph, and the Child. Taking Jesus in his arms he exclaimed:

"Now thou dost dismiss thy servant, O Lord, according to thy word, in peace;

Because my eyes have seen thy salvation, which thou hast prepared before the face of all peoples:

A light of revelation of the Gentiles, and a glory of thy people Israel" (Lk. 2:29–32).

His words are not lost, because the Church uses this prayer in the Breviary to close each day.

In the extraordinary form, the Feast of the Purification is also called Candlemas Day, the day of the Mass of the Candles. In earlier times the faithful held lighted candles on this day, during the Gospel and from the Consecration to the Communion.

Christ, the Light of the World, was presented in the temple on the Feast of the Purification. In memory of the event, the Church blesses the candles she will use during the year. The lighted candle is a symbol of Jesus, who is to cast out the darkness of sin. St. Anselm says that the wax is a symbol of the body of Christ, the wick, His soul, and the flame tells that He is God.

The candle stands for Christ, and is used in the liturgy wherever Christ is present. As a sacramental, it is the outward symbol of the graces God gives to us. It should be lighted by the faithful in their homes for family devotions, during storms, at the Communion of the sick, and during the administration of the Last Sacraments.

The meaning of the lighted candles may be learned best from the words of the beautiful prayer used by the priest when he blesses them:

"O Lord Jesus Christ, true Light, who gives light to every man who comes into this world, give Your blessing to these candles and sanctify them with the light of Your grace. Mercifully grant that even as these lights, set on fire by a visible flame, dispel the gloom of night, so also our hearts, made bright by an invisible fire, that is, by the splendor of the Holy Spirit, may be freed from the blindness of all vices, that the eyes of our minds being purified, we may be able to see such things as are pleasing to You and profitable to our salvation so that, after the dark perils of this life, we may attain light eternal."

FOR ME TO REVIEW

Questions

1. Are these statements true or false?
   A. St. John was known as a martyr.
   B. The Feast of the Holy Innocents shows us that even children can suffer for Christ.
   C. Jesus received His name when He was circumcised.
   D. St. Stephen shows us the courage a Christian needs to live like Christ.
   E. St. Stephen is sometimes called the Apostle of Love.
   F. The Holy Innocents were the first to give their lives for the Christ Child.
   G. When He was circumcised, Christ gave us an example of obedience and suffering.
2. Fill in the blank spaces, using the following words:

Christmas	Holy Spirit	Son
Father	Epiphany	Gold
Divinity	miracle	
prayer	obedience	

   A. Frankincense is a symbol of . . . .
   B. God the . . . . . . said, "This is my beloved . . . . . . , in whom I am well pleased."

C. At the marriage-feast at Cana Christ worked His first . . . .
D. At Christ's baptism in the Jordan, the . . . . . . appeared as a Dove.
E. The Feast of the Holy Family teaches us the importance of . . . .
F. . . . . . . was the gift offered to the Christ Child because He was a King.
G. When Christ changed water into wine He revealed His . . . . . . to His disciples.

FOR ME TO REMEMBER

1. St. Stephen, the first martyr, shows us how to be courageous for Christ.
2. St. John the Apostle, in his great love of Christ and of his neighbor, shows us how to live with Christ in His Church.
3. The Holy Innocents glorified God by their death.
4. Christ gave us an example of obedience when He was circumcised on the eighth day after His birth.
5. *Epiphany* means "to make known" or a "showing." Christ shows Himself to all nations as the Son of God.
6. The liturgy of the Feast of the Epiphany shows Christ as God at His baptism in the Jordan and at the Miracle at Cana.
7. In the Feast of the Holy Family the Church reminds us of a perfect example of family life.
8. The Feast of the Purification is a feast of our Lord and of the Blessed Virgin. It teaches us to be humble and obedient as they were.

FOR ME TO DO

1. Discuss ways in which we can apply the lessons learned from the liturgy of this Christmas Season.
2. Dramatize some scene from the life of a modern St. Stephen.
3. Make an all-over pattern using the Chi-Rho symbol for the name of Jesus.
4. Dramatize a modern version of the story of the adoration of the Magi. Make the costumes for each of the Wise Men.
5. Make a collage showing the important events in the early childhood of Christ. Parallel it with a collage showing modern children imitating Christ.
6. Create a poster about the Holy Family. Make a 3D-model of their home in Nazareth.
7. Read about the life of Jesus when He was a little boy. Study pictures of Him helping Mary and Joseph.
8. Give examples of honor, love, and help toward parents.
9. Copy a prayer for parents from an approved source or make up a short one and recite it often for them.
10. Study the following pictures:
    The Holy Family by El Greco
    The Boy Christ in the Temple by Hofman
11. Make greeting cards or bookmarks for the Feast of the Three Kings. Use symbols showing the true meaning of the day.

Summary of Unit 4

The first part of the Church Year—the Christmas Cycle—extends from the First Sunday of Advent to just before Lent. During its early phase, Advent (which means "coming") we prepare, with St. John the Baptist and the Blessed Virgin, for the coming Redeemer. We make ourselves as worthy as possible of Him.

On Christmas Day itself the entire Church rejoices with the angels and shepherds over the birth of the God-Man, Jesus Christ. On this day each priest is allowed to offer three Masses.

The feasts right after Christmas—those of St. Stephen, of St. John the Apostle, and of the Holy Innocents—teach us how we must serve the infant Jesus. On the Epiphany, Jesus showed His glory to the Magi who represented the people of the whole world.

Let us now journey with Christ through the Lenten season, where He will finish His work of redemption.

Write your answers on a separate sheet of paper

Part 1 Use each word in a sentence

Gentile	martyr	sanctifying grace
Immaculate	prophet	miracle
precursor	Advent	antiphon

Part 2 Multiple Choice

Choose the one answer that makes each statement correct.

1. The best way to prepare for the coming of Christ is by:
   A. doing daily little acts of sacrifice.
   B. making a Christmas novena.
   C. preparing an Advent Wreath.
2. We imitate Mary best in her preparation for Christmas when we:
   A. wear her medal every day.
   B. sing and pray in her honor.
   C. do what God wants us to do, as she did.
3. The best way to learn to live with Christ is:
   A. through the Liturgy.
   B. by reading books on the life of Christ.
   C. by studying our religion lessons.
4. St. John the Baptist preached to the people primarily to:
   A. prove that he was the forerunner of Christ.
   B. prepare their hearts and minds for the coming of the Savior.
   C. encourage them to leave home and to live in the desert.
5. We put Christ first in everything we do by:
   A. reciting carefully our morning prayers.
   B. putting money in the collection basket.
   C. imitating the virtues of Christ.

Part 3 What are the lessons for our lives which can be learned from:

1. The Solemnity of Mary?
2. The Epiphany?
3. The Feast of the Holy Family?
4. The Baptism of our Lord?

UNIT

5 Living With Christ in His Church—Easter Cycle

We believe in the Redemption. We believe that Christ, by His Passion and death, helped man to raise himself from sin to supernatural life, restoring what should have been according to God's plan.

In the Easter Cycle, the Redemption will be the center of our thoughts and actions. As members of Christ's Mystical Body, we live in and with Christ during His Passion and death, in His glorious Resurrection, and in His Ascension into heaven.

The celebration of the birth of Christ and the founding of His Kingdom now gives way to a time of sorrow and penance. We are ready to begin a new season. During this time Christ will show He is God, conquer sin, and complete the work of our redemption.

The Church, like a good Mother, knows that we have been celebrating Christ's coming with joy and happiness, and that we will find it hard to change to a season of sadness and penance all at once. She paves the way little by little in the liturgy, as she goes from the season of Christmas to that of Easter.

The Easter Season is the second part of the great drama of our redemption. It is preceded by a season of preparation, Lent; followed by a season of application, Pentecost. Within the season of Lent there are six Sundays. We follow carefully our Lord's struggle with death, sin, and suffering.

CHAPTER 17

Living With Christ During Lent

The Meaning and Spirit of Lent

If we really live in the spirit of the liturgy, we will give our wills and minds and bodies to Christ that He might continue His work of redemption in the world today, through us. He needs our hands and bodies, our minds and wills, to do His holy work: to pray with Him, to do penance with Him, to suffer, yes, and to die with Him.

We now enter a period of penance and prayer with Christ. The Church echoes Christ's call more clearly than ever before: "If anyone wishes to come after me, let him deny himself, and take up his cross, and follow me" (Mt. 16:24).

Before beginning His Public Life, Christ stayed in the desert for forty days and forty nights fasting, praying, and suffering all kinds of discomforts. Jesus was perfect, without sin. He did not have to do penance. Yet He wanted to give us an example. What a Model for us to have! During the forty days of Lent Christ's Mystical Body unites the sufferings of its members with those of its Head, Christ. The Church wishes us to die to self and our own desires so that we may rise with Him to a new life on Easter Sunday.

Now the question arises—what sacrifices can we make during Lent? There are many from which to choose. We may give up something we like—candy, movies, or social media—and give more of our time and resources to the Church and to those in need. We can give up our own selfish desires in order to do

Christ's will, making special efforts to be kind and patient with our brothers and sisters, our classmates, and to be obedient to our parents and teachers. We can make the Stations of the Cross or a visit to the Blessed Sacrament every day; we can help the poor, the sick, the blind, the ignorant, especially sinners and those who do not know Christ. No matter how small the sacrifice is, our Savior will be pleased if it is done cheerfully and for the love of Him.

"If anyone wishes to come after me, let him deny himself, and take up his cross, and follow me" (Mt. 16:24).

In addition, there is one offering we can make which is perfect in itself, the Mass, in which Christ offers Himself to His heavenly Father. Each time we devoutly attend Mass, united with the Mystical Body of Christ, we offer the heavenly Father this priceless gift. We sometimes think that because other sacrifices are harder they might be greater. But we must never forget that in the Mass our sacrifice is united to Christ's, which is of infinite value.

Lent is a time for turning away from all that is displeasing to God. It is a "coming back" to God, to His divine Son and His Church. It is a "coming back" to the teachings of the Church and the sacraments. Lent is a season during which, with the help of almighty God, we try to make holy our thoughts, words, and actions. It is a period also in which we strive to gain grace for others as well as for ourselves.

If we are faithful in following the spirit of Lent, our lives will begin to take on a supernatural power and beauty which comes from living with Christ. Then God will not deal with us according to our sins, but according to His great mercy. And He will also allow His graces to flow to others who need them very much.

We are adopted children of God. This is our good fortune! Think of the millions of people who have not been so blessed. We should often think of God's great favors to us, especially during Lent. At the same time, we should thank Him for it. Lent is the time to remember our Baptism. It is also a time to remember that one day we shall die and rise again.

In the early Church, the ceremonies of Baptism were carried out one by one from the beginning of Lent to the night before Easter. The whole period of time was a time of final testing and examination for those who were to become members of the Catholic Church through Baptism on Easter Sunday.

Ash Wednesday

Would you be surprised to see the news on the first day of Lent and see in the headlines: "*Christians Declare War on Enemies of Salvation*"? If such an unusual thing should happen, the article might go on to read as follows: "Holy Mother Church is urging all members of the Mystical Body to join forces with their Leader, Christ. The weapons to be used are prayer and penance. The battle will be fierce, but with Christ on our side victory is certain. Each soldier is asked to obey Christ exactly and to come to the altar as often as possible to receive the necessary strength from the Eucharistic sacrifice. Daily instructions as to the plan of battle may also be had."

Does this sound impossible? Yet every bit of it is true. During the past year we may have allowed ourselves to drift away somewhat from Christ. We may have been too attached to certain things to remember that we are not to live in this world forever.

The Church wishes to remind us that heaven is to be sought with all our might, and the time to act is *now.* On Ash Wednesday she places this thought before our minds in an impressive ceremony. Before Mass on that day, ashes, made by burning last year's palms, are blessed. Then after Mass they are placed on each person's forehead in the form of a cross while the following words are recited:

"Remember, you are dust and to dust you will return." The ashes wear away before the day is over but the thought must remain imprinted on our minds.

The Lord is the best instructor on what is needed for a good and holy Lent. Let us look at what He says in the Gospel of Matthew: "Do not lay up for yourselves treasures on earth . . . but lay up for yourselves treasures in heaven" (Mt. 6:19, 20). Each kind thought we have or deed we do for the love of God is a beautiful jewel for heaven's treasure chest.

There is another important idea brought out in the Gospel: "When you fast, anoint your head and wash your face, so that you may not be seen by men to fast, but by your Father, who is in secret; and your Father, who sees in secret, will reward you" (Mt. 6:17–18). What does this mean? A good intention is necessary for reaping the spiritual fruits of prayer. Jesus tells us above, for instance, that if we pray only to make others think we are "prayerful" then we receive only the "reward" of vain self-righteousness, while we forfeit the rewards of true prayer.

Like the crippled servant in the Gospel, we can do nothing by ourselves. We send for Christ, and our Redeemer says: "I will come and cure him." On Ash Wednesday we turn to Christ in penance. In the Gospel we again see the centurion telling Christ about his servant's sickness. Christ promises to cure him. And so also, as we learn in Lent, Christ will come to cure and save those who call on Him and listen to His directions of prayer and penance.

Our holy Mother the Church tells us how we can do penance. She commands us *to fast and to abstain on the days appointed.* "To abstain" means "to keep away." Days on which we are to keep away from eating meat are called "days of abstinence." A "day of fasting" is a day where we limit the amount of food we eat, eating less than we usually would according to what the Church requires.

Remember, you are dust and to dust you will return.

Ash Wednesday and Good Friday are obligatory days of fasting and abstinence (from meat) for those aged 18 to 59. The day of fasting allows for one full meal, though two smaller meals (both of them together not adding up to more than a full meal) may also be consumed. In addition, Catholics aged 14 and older must abstain from meat on all Fridays during Lent. Note that there are exemptions from these requirements for those who are in special circumstances, like those who are ill, or are pregnant. If you have any questions or concerns about following the requirements, bring them up to an adult or a trusted member of your parish. Children are not obliged to fast because they are still growing and need food to build strong and healthy bodies. Instead, they should make other sacrifices, for instance, replacing some time that you might usually spend playing games with a time of prayer or spiritual reading.

By fasting and abstaining we can unite ourselves to Christ and gain the strength to stay close to Him all our lives. Practicing difficult virtues is so much easier if we become used to saying "no" to ourselves now and then in small things. For such reasons, beyond adhering to the obligatory days of fasting and abstinence mentioned above, all Catholics are encouraged to freely give up something of their own choosing during the forty days of Lent. We often call this practice our "Lenten resolution," since we personally ***resolve*** to give up something. Now, Christians are *always* to be putting away sin, so Lent is as good a time as any other to redouble our efforts against sin. But specifically during Lent, what we choose to give up should generally be something that is good, something that it is not necessarily a vice, but which we have a regular habit of enjoying (e.g., eating out at our favorite restaurant, using social media throughout the day); the idea is to sacrifice something good for the sake of Him who is infinitely greater than any other good thing, Jesus Christ.

Our weapons are ready, we have our instructions. Christ our Leader is strong, and the victory of Easter Sunday is in sight. The amount of joy we experience at the Resurrection will, in part, be measured by the sacrifices made during Lent.

The First Sunday of Lent

The following prayer has been used by the Church at the start of Lent for more than 1,500 years. It helps to clarify the purpose of our good works:

> *"O God, You purify Your Church every year by a fast of forty days. Grant to Your people the perfection they strive to obtain from You by their abstinence, and let it be manifest in the good works which they perform."*

Let us begin the study of this Sunday by asking a few personal questions. How do you feel about those sacrifices you usually choose to offer during Lent? Are you quickly discouraged? Does it not seem as though forty days is a very long time to fight against your worldly desires? After all, why should we deny ourselves so many things when many people are forgetting all about Lent and Christ's sufferings?

If some of these questions make you want to nod "Yes" it could be that you are being tempted. But do not worry. Temptations will come to all of us. Even Christ allowed the devil to tempt Him, to show us that through Him, and by His example, we are able to resist every temptation.

During Lent the Church tells us the story of Christ's temptations after He spent forty days and forty nights without eating or drinking. She wants us to learn from Christ's example.

At the end of the forty days Jesus was weak from hunger and

thirst. The devil came to Him and tempted Him to change the stones into something to eat. The devil tries to tempt us, too, to give up our Lenten resolutions for something that is more pleasant.

Satan saw that Christ was not going to give in to this temptation. He, therefore, tried to tempt Him to become proud. He dared Him to show His power by throwing Himself from the top of the temple. Sometimes Satan also tempts us to think we are better than others because of our good works, like our sacrifices during Lent. Needless to say, the devil failed when he tried to tempt Christ in this way.

The devil made one last try. This time he tempted our Lord to give up His heavenly kingdom for an earthly one, just as he often tempts us to forget about heaven and enjoy ourselves here on earth. What was Christ's reply? "Begone, Satan!" He said, and the devil, knowing that it was useless to try any longer, left our Lord and the "angels came and ministered to him" (Mt. 4:1–11).

What a useful lesson for us! To carry out God's plan for us now and hereafter means that we must keep up with our Lenten sacrifices, trying to grow more like Jesus Christ. If we are faithful in our penance, we will overcome the devil. However, we cannot handle the devil alone. He is much smarter than we are. But if we imitate and stay close to Christ and ask His help, the devil will not be able to succeed.

Keeping close to Christ includes receiving Him frequently and devoutly in Holy Communion. In this sacrament we become one with Christ; and Christ, working through us, will give us the power to do things we could not possibly do alone. Holy Mother Church realizes how much we need Christ's help. That is why she insists that all Catholics receive Holy Communion at least once during the Easter season.

Do not, however, be content with receiving Holy Communion only once during that time. For closeness to Christ and strength to follow Him, we need His help. Where better can we gain this than in Holy Communion? Frequent, even daily Communion, is one of the best Lenten practices of virtue. It requires love of Christ, courage, and perseverance.

The Second Sunday of Lent

Christ knows we need encouragement when we are asked to persevere in doing a difficult and distasteful task. So He has His Church encourage us on the second Sunday of Lent. He gives us a glimpse of the happiness He has promised those who serve Him faithfully.

Have you ever wondered what heaven is like? Suppose this morning you were told that before nightfall you might have one peek into heaven. Would you be excited? Surely! Do you think your life would change after that grand experience? How would it be changed? To strengthen our resolves to continue our penances the Church presents the story of the Transfiguration on the second Sunday of Lent to give us an idea of the glory that awaits those who do penance with Christ.

Peter, James, and John walked with Christ to the top of a small mountain. There, before their very eyes, a wonderful thing happened. Christ was transfigured; He was changed! The Gospel of Matthew tells us, "And his face shone as the sun, and his garments became white as snow" (Mt. 17:2). Not only this, but Elijah and Moses appeared next to Christ and were talking with Him (Mk 9:4). How thrilled the Apostles must have been at the sight of the indescribable beauty and the dazzling majesty of their Lord and Leader!

Up to that time the Apostles had seen Christ only as man. Christ knew that during the months to come, and especially during His Passion, the Apostles would have to fight many temptations and hardships for His sake. So, He encouraged them by letting them see Him in some of His divine glory.

The Church wants us to think often of the greatness of the King to whom we are now offering little acts of self-denial. We have often heard stories of people doing brave deeds for the sake of an earthly leader. How much prouder we should be to offer our daily sacrifices, so pleasing to the heart of the King of kings. If we serve Him, our bodies will be glorified too. During the remaining weeks of Lent let us keep this thought before us: If we are faithful in our penances during Lent, Christ will reward us by allowing us to share in His glory in heaven. Then, too, if we receive Holy Communion frequently and devoutly, we can share in the Transfiguration. We become one with Christ through an increase of divine life. "It is now no longer I that live, but Christ lives in me" (Gal. 2:20). It is good for us to remember that the Transfiguration is another proof that Jesus Christ is truly God. He will never fail in His promises.

Third Sunday of Lent

During this third week of Lent, it is well to meditate on the story of Joseph who was sold into slavery by his brothers (Gen. 37). Joseph is a "type" of Christ because the character and situation of Joseph have certain similarities to Jesus. In the same manner, we fallen people are like Joseph's sinful brothers. But Christ saves us despite our sinfulness, even as Joseph saved his brothers despite their terrible sins against them. Christ wants to save us, and He will, if only we turn to Him and use His grace.

Have you ever played "Tug of War"? Suppose that on one team there was a boy who decided he would do no pulling at all. Would he be helping his team? Would he be helping the other team? This is the same idea Christ had in mind when He spoke these words: "He who is not with me is against me" (Lk. 11:23). In other words, those who are not working on Christ's side are by that very fact helping Satan's army and working against Christ. Christ wants to redeem all men, but only those who love and serve Him will be saved.

If we are faithful followers of Jesus it is not enough merely to avoid doing evil. We must "put on Jesus Christ" and try each day to grow in holiness and virtue. Instead of saying, "I will not be unkind or disobedient," go further and say, "I shall try to do as many kind acts as possible and obey cheerfully for the love of Christ." So you see how your life will begin to be patterned after that of Christ, who spent His whole life doing good.

Through Baptism and the Holy Eucharist, Christ overcomes the devil in each one of us. We have passed from darkness to light, Christ is our light, and, as His Apostle Paul tells us, we are to "Walk, then, as children of light (for the fruit of the light is in all goodness and justice and truth)" (Eph. 5:9).

On the first Sunday of Lent, we signed up as active members in Christ's army. As the season of Lent continues, it will become more necessary to unite with Christ if we are to win a victory over Satan's forces. Christ is a gentle but strong leader. He takes on the hardest jobs Himself and is always ready to come to our help at once. When we follow such a leader, we can be sure of victory.

Fourth Sunday of Lent (Laetare Sunday)

The fourth Sunday, or middle Sunday of Lent, is a special day in the Church Year. You will discover this as you attend Mass. Flowers, absent from the altar since the beginning of Lent, may decorate it once more for today only. The priest saying Mass may use rose-colored vestments instead of the usual violet ones of penance. The Mass begins with the Latin word *laetare* which means "Rejoice!" You may wonder why we should rejoice in Lent. The Church rejoices because Lent is half over. Our redemption is near! Easter with its great victory of life over death is almost here!

> *"Lent is the Autumn of the spiritual life during which we gather fruit to keep us going for the rest of the year."*
>
> —*St. Francis de Sales*

You get excited when you realize that you are winning a game or race. You try even harder. Why should not the Church also rejoice when she realizes how close we are to the great triumph of the feast of the Resurrection? Why should she not cheer us on?

On this Sunday we should promise our Lord that we will continue in our sacrifices. If we have failed in our resolution, today is a good day to begin again. Ask our Lord to help you remain firm in your sacrifices and good works. Never give up.

There is another and better reason why there is a thread of happiness running through the liturgy today. In the early days of the Church, the vigil of Easter was the date set for the baptism of the catechumens (persons wishing to be Christians). They were happy at the thought of their approaching baptism, and the Church as a true mother rejoiced with them. On this day early Christians used to present fresh roses to the joyful catechumens. In memory of this the pope still blesses a gold rose or a bunch of roses each Laetare Sunday.

The joy on Laetare Sunday can be compared to our happiness in spring, when all nature begins to reawaken. But as the branches in a tree receive life from the roots, so the members of the Mystical Body must be united with Christ, the true Vine, in order to gain a glorious resurrection and union with God in glory in heaven.

Fifth Sunday of Lent

The fifth Sunday of Lent is also known as the first Sunday of the Passion in the extraordinary form. On this Sunday when you go to Mass you will see all the statues and crucifixes covered with violet cloth. Violet, as you already know, is the color of penance and of sorrow. Mother Church wants to show her deep sorrows for the many sins that caused the sufferings and death of Christ. She wants us to make sacrifices and to do penance for our sins. Most of all, she wants us to re-live with Christ the last days of His earthly life. She urges us saying: If we suffer with Christ we shall be glorified together with Him. And she presents Christ as speaking to us and saying that those of us who keep His word will not taste death forever.

The Church presents for our meditation Christ the High Priest, the sinless One, who will wash away our sins with His blood.

The Gospels tell us that many hated Christ, and falsely accused Him of wrongdoing. Jesus asked them to try to prove that He had committed any sin. When they could not, He told them: "Amen, amen, I say to you, before Abraham came to be, I am" (Jn. 8:58). Jesus meant, "I have lived from all eternity." Since God alone had no beginning, Jesus was telling them that He is God. These people got angry and took up stones to throw at our Lord but He hid from them. His time had not yet come.

Although our attention is drawn to the wickedness of Christ's enemies, still the thought of Easter shines through: "Abraham your father rejoiced that he might see my day."

On this Sunday, more than ever, the Holy Eucharist is a "living" memorial of Christ's dreadful death on the cross.

It is now especially that we make a petition for unfailing help from Christ to suffer with, in, and through Him.

During this week (traditionally called "Passion Week") the

Masses present many thoughts which help us join with Christ in His sufferings. Daniel in the lions' den reminds us of Christ descending into the den of sinners. The story of the woman anointing Christ's feet makes us think of Christ's coming death and encourages us to serve Christ as she did, even if we are sinners as she was.

Holy Week

Holy Week is the most solemn week in the whole Church Year! It is the greatest and the holiest! During this week all the liturgical prayers, hymns, and readings are filled not only with the remembrances of our Lord's sufferings and death, to spur us on to join Him in His Passion, but also with a note of joy, looking toward the Easter victory.

Holy Week begins with Palm Sunday and ends with Holy Saturday.

Palm Sunday

Palm Sunday is the "gateway to Holy Week." Its liturgy expresses both joy and sorrow.

On the first Palm Sunday the men, women, and children who followed Jesus into Jerusalem threw flowers and palm branches at His feet and hailed Him as their King. This was the day when He, "the desired of all nations, came unto his own." However, at the end of that same week the people's tribute turned to hatred and Jesus began another procession—His Way of the Cross.

As we hold the blessed palm on Sunday and hear the joyous words of the song "Hosanna to the Son of David! Blessed is He who comes in the name of the Lord! Hosanna in the highest!" we are glad to show the world our deep faith in Christ, the greatest of kings. This is a good time to renew our promise to live for God and ask Him to grant us perseverance. We can enter heaven only if we serve Christ faithfully.

We should keep the blessed palm in our homes to remind us every day that Jesus Christ is our King. The palm is a sacramental which can help us to receive, and cooperate with, grace. It will help to give us strength to overcome sin. Do you recall what a sacramental is? Can you name other sacramentals?

During this Mass and throughout all of Holy Week, it is well to consider three important aspects of our Lord's Passion. First, Christ became "obedient to death, even to death on a cross" (Phil. 2:8). For this reason, "God also has exalted him and has bestowed upon him the name that is above every name, so that at the name of Jesus every knee should bend of those in heaven, on earth and under the earth" (Phil. 2:9–10). Holy Week can help us learn this lesson of Christ's obedience, so that we may practice it every day of our lives and finally share with Christ in His resurrection.

The second important thought is Christ's struggle to free man from the powers of the devil. We must join our King in the fight against sin in ourselves and in the world. In Baptism we receive divine life; we, therefore, fight with Christ's strength and power and can share in His great victory over sin and death.

The third thought is that of our Lord's great sufferings and death and His great trust in His heavenly Father. Christ looked forward to His Resurrection, and to the joy of seeing the human race redeemed to give glory to God for all times.

During Holy Week this year let us beg Jesus Christ to teach us how to join our little sufferings with His. We should also ask Him to increase our trust in God and to help us obey His will at all times. Then, surely, we shall share in Christ's victory.

Holy Thursday

Holy Thursday is one of the important days in the life of our Lord Jesus Christ. It is also important for the life of His Mystical Body.

On Holy Thursday Jesus instituted the Holy Eucharist as a sacrament and a sacrifice, giving us the Mass and Holy Communion as His parting gift. On this day Jesus also instituted the sacrament of Holy Orders and made His Apostles the first priests.

He gave them, as well as all the priests of the Church, the power to celebrate Mass and to change bread and wine into His sacred Body and Blood.

The Mass *commemorates* the Last Supper of Christ on earth and is celebrated sometime between five and eight o'clock in the evening. When the "Gloria" is intoned all the bells of the Church are rung joyously. They are not heard again until the "Gloria" of Holy Saturday, for the Church now goes into deep mourning, since the death of Christ is near at hand.

The readings for Holy Thursday tell us about the institution of the Sacrifice of the Mass and the sacrament of Holy Eucharist as well as their prefigurement in Exodus 12:1–8. Paul reminds his converts that our Lord, "on the night in which he was betrayed, took bread, and giving thanks broke, and said, 'This is my body which shall be given up for you; do this in remembrance of me.' In like manner also the cup, after he had supped, saying, 'This cup is the new covenant in my blood; do this as often as you drink it, in remembrance of me'" (1 Cor. 11:23–25).

The Gospel for the day shows us how Christ, our Lord and Redeemer, offered us a perfect example of humility. After the Last Supper, John tells us in his Gospel, Jesus humbly washed the feet of His Apostles. When Peter protested that this was not right, our Lord said to him: "If I do not wash thee, thou shalt have no part with me" (Jn. 13:8). This shows us that it is Christ the Lord who cleanses us from sin.

When He had finished, Jesus spoke to His Apostles, saying: "Do you know what I have done to you? You call me Master and Lord, and you say well, for so I am. If, therefore, I the Lord and Master have washed your feet, you also ought to wash the feet of one another. For I have given you an example, that as I have done to you, so you also should do" (Jn. 13:12–15). This example of Christ is practiced on Holy Thursday. Traditionally, after the Mass at the cathedral, the bishop washes the feet of his assistants. This shows that the bishop takes the place of Christ in his diocese, and that, like Christ, he takes fatherly care of us, the members of the Mystical Body. Many priests implement this tradition at their parish as well. At times you will hear people refer to Holy Thursday as Maundy Thursday. The word *maundy* means "wash", and this goes back to Christ's example of washing the feet of His Apostles.

After the Sacrifice of the Mass is finished, the Blessed Sacrament is carried in solemn procession to the side altar. During the procession the "Pange Lingua" is traditionally sung, which is a beautiful Eucharistic hymn written by St. Thomas Aquinas.

The services end with the stripping of the altars, to show that the Sacrifice of the Mass is interrupted and will not be offered until Christ is risen from the dead. What can we think about while the altar is being stripped? We can recall how Christ was stripped of everything—His garments, His glory, and His friends. Should we resolve to strip ourselves of those things which keep us from practicing and showing forth the virtues of Christ?

Every Holy Thursday, Mother Church wants us to remember the wonderful gifts Jesus Christ gave us on this day. She asks us to make visits to our Lord in the Blessed Sacrament, and if possible, to receive Holy Communion. That is the best way to thank Jesus for giving Himself to us as our food. Can you do this for Jesus? He will be waiting for you on Holy Thursday.

Traditionally on Holy Thursday a special ceremony takes place in every cathedral church called "The Chrism Mass." The Holy Oils are blessed by the bishop. The Church uses three different Holy Oils—the Oil of the Sick, the Oil of the Catechumens, and the Holy Chrism. When is each of these Holy Oils used?

Good Friday

Did you ever wonder when God showed His love for you most? Of course, God loves you without limit all the time; but on your baptismal day and on your First Holy Communion Day, for example, God showed a special love for you. He showed in a very strong and clear way how very much He loves you.

In the Church Year there are two days that could very well be called days of God's special love. These two days are Holy Thursday and Good Friday. Both of these days are filled with a spirit of love. When Christ celebrated the Passover at the Last Supper on Holy

Thursday, it served as a preparation for the bloody sacrifice of the cross.

In the liturgy the Church shows the close connection between Holy Thursday and Good Friday. On Holy Thursday we celebrate the institution of the Blessed Sacrament. On Good Friday there is no Mass. Instead, we have a special service which is divided into four parts: the Liturgy of the Word, the Solemn Intercessions, the Adoration of the Cross, and the Communion Service.

> *"The Cross is the way of Paradise, but only when it's borne willingly."*
>
> *—St. Paul of the Cross*

Liturgy of the Word

During this part of the service the readings, responsories, and collects recall how Judas betrayed Jesus to the Jews, and how Jesus died on the cross between two thieves. The readings fill us with hope in the resurrection of Christ. Then follows the beautiful account of the Passion of our Lord, in which St. John presents to us the suffering Savior as King and God. As we stand to listen to St. John's Gospel, we would do well to join in spirit with the Blessed Mother and the others standing at the foot of the cross.

Solemn Intercessions

At the end of the first part of the Good Friday service, prayers are said for all people because Christ died for all men. To please God, we too must pray and offer sacrifices for everybody, even our enemies.

The Adoration of the Cross

The third part of the Good Friday service is the veneration of the cross. We venerate the crucifix and offer to Christ crucified our sorrowful hearts, asking Him to offer us in and with His own sacrifice today.

The priest lays aside his cope and begins to take off the violet veil covering the crucifix. Each time a part of the crucifix is uncovered, the priest sings, "Behold the wood of the Cross on which hung the Savior of the world." The people kneel and answer, "Come, let us adore."

Then the priest approaches the crucifix genuflecting three times at different distances. He then kisses the wounds of Christ Crucified, to honor the Redeemer and the cross– the sign of our salvation. The people also venerate and kiss Christ's holy cross.

The sacred liturgy continues with the hymns of lamentation or complaints made by our Lord to His people, who have been and still are ungrateful and unfaithful to God. "What more should I have done for you, and have not done." "I have raised you up with great power, and you have hung me on the gibbet of the cross."

Beg God to deepen our sorrow for our sins, which continually crucify Jesus in His Mystical Body, and to grant us the grace truly to die to sin and to all that is evil.

Communion Service

The last ceremony of the day is the Communion service, in which we can unite ourselves sacramentally with our Lord on the cross.

On Good Friday Jesus Christ died on the cross to redeem us and all men. For every Christian it is the saddest day of the year, and yet we call it "good." Have you ever wondered why?

It is, indeed, good for us! By His sufferings and death, Jesus earned grace for us and gave us the means to win heaven! Through the cross joy came to the world.

Our Lord led the way that we might be brave and strong to follow His bloody footsteps up Mount Calvary, there to crucify ourselves with Him. We can do this by faithfully keeping Christ's law of love, by putting Him first in our thoughts and by avoiding sin. Mary, Christ's Mother and ours, will teach us how to suffer with her divine Son. She stood beneath the cross when Jesus was hanging on it and suffered along with Him. But more important, day by day, she cheerfully and patiently offered up the little trials and sufferings of life. All of us can do this for our Lord. She allowed no created good to come between her and her Son. Do we?

Holy Saturday

On Holy Saturday our Lord rested in the tomb. The spirit of the whole day is one of deep recollection and of great inner sorrow. The liturgy of this day is the rich and meaningful liturgy of the Easter Vigil. The resurrection of Christ is the main point of the service. In spirit, it helps us re-live the glorious victory of the resurrection of Christ and our own spiritual resurrection from the slavery of sin as Christ comes to live in each one of us. Through Baptism we rose from the death of sin to the life of sanctifying grace. We become one with Christ. Therefore, all self-love and self-will must be erased so that Christ may work and grow in us.

The ceremonies of the Holy Saturday Easter Virgil in the ordinary form are:

1. The Service of Light.
2. Liturgy of the Word.
3. Liturgy of Baptism.
4. Liturgy of the Eucharist.

In the extraordinary form, the ceremonies differ slightly in name and content, but generally follow the same structure.

The Service of Light

The Easter Vigil begins with the blessing of the new fire. A blazing fire is prepared in a suitable place outside the church. When the people are gathered there, the priest approaches with the ministers, one of whom carries the Paschal Candle. After the fire is blessed, the priest blesses five red grains of incense, which are put into the Paschal Candle in the form of a cross. These grains of incense represent the five glorious wounds of Our Savior. The priest lights the Paschal Candle from the new fire, saying: "May the light of Christ rising in glory dispel the darkness of our hearts and minds." Then the candle is blessed.

The Paschal Candle is a special symbol of the risen Savior and is, therefore, lighted during Mass until the feast of the Ascension. It makes us think of Jesus living with us during the Easter season. It makes us remember that we, like Christ, must be a light of goodness in a sinful world.

A solemn procession forms after the lighting of the Paschal Candle. The priest, dressed in white vestments as the first sign of our Easter joy and happiness, takes the lighted Paschal Candle and carries it through the dark church in procession.

During this procession we are given a picture of how the Light of Christ is spread throughout the whole world. First, the candle held by the priest is lighted from the Paschal Candle, then the candles of those taking part in the procession. At last, the candles held by all the faithful are lighted, and the lights of the Church are turned on. This shows us how we, the members of Christ's Mystical Body, must be alight with the Light of Christ and help spread it by a good and holy life among all men.

After the procession, the priest sings the beautiful Easter song of the Church, "The Easter Proclamation" (or the *"Exsultet"*):

> "Exult, let them exult, the hosts of heaven,
> exult, let Angel ministers of God exult,
> let the trumpet of salvation
> sound aloud our mighty King's triumph!
>
> ...This is the night,
> when Christ broke the prison-bars of death
> and rose victorious from the underworld...
>
> ... O wonder of your humble care for us!
> O love, O charity beyond all telling,
> to ransom a slave you gave away your Son!
> O truly necessary sin of Adam,
> destroyed completely by the Death of Christ!
> O happy fault
> that earned so great, so glorious a Redeemer..."

After blessing the new fire and the Paschal Candle we turn to the second part of the Easter Vigil.

Liturgy of the Word

Seven readings from the Old Testament and two readings from the New Testament are chosen to recount important moments in salvation history. The readings are a short review of the story of man—from the creation of the world to the redemption. These readings also remind us of the many graces which we receive from the sacrament of Baptism and which help us remain faithful to God. After the seven Old Testament readings, all are quiet until the priest intones the Gloria. Then the organ sounds and joins the jubilant ringing of the bells to announce the glory and joy of Easter to the whole world. After the Gloria, the first of the New Testament readings is read, followed by the Alleluia and the Gospel. The priest solemnly sings the Alleluia three times, raising his voice by a step each time, with all repeating it. The Alleluia has not been said or sung throughout all of Lent; what joy to finally proclaim it during this Easter night!

Liturgy of Baptism

The blessing of the baptismal water takes place in the form of a preface similar to the preface of the Mass. It is accompanied by ceremonies which have deep meaning.

The priest, dividing the water in the sign of the cross, breathes three times upon it, asking God to bless it and begging the Holy Spirit to take possession of it. He then dips the Paschal Candle into the water three times and prays: "May the power of the Holy Spirit descend into the well-filled font." The Holy Oils are now poured into the water to complete the blessing. The priest begs God's grace and the blessing of holy Church.

At this time, if there are any converts who wish to be baptized, the sacrament is administered to them. They rise from a life of sin to share in Christ's life. Then all present renew their Baptismal promises and, with the priest, recite the Lord's prayer and sing the Litany of the Saints. Then follows the Liturgy of the

Eucharist, in which Christ comes to the members of His Body in Holy Communion.

Liturgy of the Eucharist

The Church is filled with joy! In it the newness and glory of the Resurrection and that of the newly baptized find happy expression. In the Mass we ask God to help the newly baptized to carry out their Christian duties perfectly. The readings encourage them and, indeed, all of us to live for Christ alone, "Therefore, if you have been raised together with Christ, seek the things that are above" (Colossians 3:1).

Let us join Mother Church in thanking God for the sacraments of Baptism and the Holy Eucharist, which have made it possible for us to pass from the death of sin to the life of sanctifying grace.

In the Gospel, St. Matthew brings to us the message of the first Easter. With Mary Magdalen and "the other Mary" we come at early dawn on Easter morning to see the sepulcher and to hear the angel's message. Even more importantly, we receive our glorified Eucharistic Lord in Holy Communion.

To the *"Ite, missa est"* at the end of the Easter Virgil Mass is added a double, solemn *"Alleluia, Alleluia",* and we leave the church filled with the joy and grace and happiness of Easter. In us, as once in the newly baptized, Christ has come to live, to make us "other Christs."

If you have never joined Christ and His Church in the Holy Saturday Easter Vigil or the Holy Week services before, be sure to do it this year. But prepare yourself so you will know each part. Then you will truly rejoice on Holy Saturday and on Easter Sunday and be ready to live as disciples of Christ in the days to follow.

FOR ME TO REVIEW

Catechism Lesson

102. **Q. Which are the chief effects of the Redemption?**
A. The chief effects of the Redemption are two: The satisfaction of God's justice by Christ's sufferings and death, and the gaining of grace for men.

83. **Q. Why did Christ suffer and die?**
A. Christ suffered and died for our sins.

84. **Q. What lessons do we learn from the sufferings and death of Christ?**
A. From the sufferings and death of Christ we learn the great evil of sin, the hatred God bears to it, and the necessity of satisfying for it.

85. **Q. Where did Christ's soul go after His death?**
A. After Christ's death His soul descended into hell.

86. **Q. Did Christ's soul descend into the hell of the damned?**
A. The hell into which Christ's soul descended was not the hell of the damned, but a place or state of rest called Limbo, where the souls of the just were waiting for Him.

393. **Q. What do you mean by fast-days?**
A. By fast-days I mean days on which we are allowed but one full meal.

394. **Q. What do you mean by days of abstinence?**
A. By days of abstinence I mean days on which we are forbidden to eat flesh-meat, but are allowed the usual number of Meals.

395. Q. Why does the Church command us to fast and abstain?

A. The Church commands us to fast and abstain, in order that we may mortify our passions and satisfy for our sins.

259. Q. When are we bound to receive Holy Communion?

A. We are bound to receive Holy Communion at least once during the Easter season.

239. Q. When did Christ institute the Holy Eucharist?

A. Christ instituted the Holy Eucharist at the Last Supper, the night before He died.

241. Q. How did our Lord institute the Holy Eucharist?

A. Our Lord instituted the Holy Eucharist by taking bread, blessing, breaking, and giving to His Apostles, saying: "Take ye and eat, This is My Body"; and then by taking the cup of wine, blessing and giving it, saying to them: "Drink ye all of this. This is My Blood which shall be shed for the remission of sins. Do this for a commemoration of Me."

242. Q. What happened when our Lord said, "This is My Body; this is My Blood?"

A. When our Lord said, "This is My Body," the substance of the bread was changed into the substance of His Body; when He said, "This is My Blood," the substance of the wine was changed into the substance of His Blood.

249. Q. When did Christ give His priests the power to change bread and wine into His Body and Blood?

A. Christ gave His priests the power to change bread and wine into His Body and Blood when He said to the Apostles, "Do this in commemoration of Me."

Questions

1. Answer these statements with YES or NO:
   A. Christ is pleased when we do little things to show Him our love.
   B. We are following Christ's example when we offer sacrifices during Lent.
   C. Lent lasts for fifty days.
   D. Lent is a preparation for the great feast of Easter.
   E. If we have been faithful in suffering with Christ during Lent, we will rise with Him to a new life on Easter Sunday.
2. Answer these questions in a few words:
   A. Why is the first day of Lent called Ash Wednesday?
   B. Where do the ashes come from that are used in the ceremony?
   C. What does the priest say as he places ashes on each forehead?
   D. How do we lay up treasures in heaven?
   E. Why should all Christians rejoice on Laetare Sunday?
   F. What are some of the signs of joy you notice in Church on this Sunday?
3. Match the following phrases with the numbers of the answers on the right.

a) Fifth Sunday of Lent	1. Blessed things or actions
b) Redemption	2. Song of Praise
c) "Hosanna"	3. Place where our Lord was crucified
d) St. Matthew's Gospel	4. Passion Sunday
e) Sacramentals	5. Sacrament and Sacrifice
f) Holy Eucharist	6. Holy Thursday
g) Maundy Thursday	7. Sufferings and death of Christ
h) Calvary	8. Read on Palm Sunday

FOR ME TO REMEMBER

1. Christ fasted and prayed in the desert for forty days. We are called to follow Christ's example of prayer and penance during the forty days of Lent.
2. The most perfect sacrifice we can offer during Lent is daily to unite ourselves devoutly with Christ at the Sacrifice of the Mass.
3. Ash Wednesday is the first day of Lent.
4. On Ash Wednesday we receive blessed ashes to remind us of the death of the body.
5. The prayer and penance we offer during Lent are meant to help us become more like Christ.
6. A temptation is not a sin.
7. Close union with Christ is the only way to reach heaven.
8. A perfect way of keeping close to Christ is to receive Him devoutly and often in Holy Communion.
9. Easter time in the United States is from Easter Sunday to Pentecost Sunday (50 days).
10. The Church wishes us all to think often of the greatness of Christ our King, to lead us on to greater acts of self-denial and devotion.
11. Faithful followers of Christ will share His glory in heaven.
12. To live a Christian life, it is not enough merely to avoid sin, we must also practice the virtues of Christ.
13. *Laetare* is a Latin word meaning "Rejoice."
14. We rejoice on the fourth Sunday of Lent because Christ's victory on Easter is almost here.

15. The priest is permitted to wear rose-colored vestments on two Sundays in the Church Year—Laetare Sunday (middle of Lent), and Gaudete Sunday (middle of Advent).
16. The blessed palms we receive on Palm Sunday are sacramentals.
17. On Holy Thursday we recall especially the institution of the sacraments of Holy Eucharist and Holy Orders.
18. The Paschal Candle is the symbol of Christ, the Light of the world.

FOR ME TO DO

1. Plan a booklet of Lenten symbols with short explanations for each.
2. Write a paragraph on "How I Can Make Lent Holy."
3. Receive Holy Communion daily, once a week, or as often as you can.
4. Arrange a presentation showing the meaning of Lent.
5. Look at pictures illustrating the institution of the Holy Eucharist. Name some of the Apostles.
6. Study the crucifix. Tell all that Jesus merited for us through the sacrifice of the cross.
7. Make plans for how we shall make our visits to the "Altar of Repose."
8. List all the things that were done by or happened to Jesus on Holy Thursday; on Good Friday.
9. Compose individual meditations on one or more of the Stations of the Cross.

10. Study the gospel story of the preparation for the Last Supper, and then dramatize a part of it.

11. Memorize the Sorrowful Mysteries of the rosary. Pray the rosary often.

12. Attend the services on Good Friday. Offer Christ your adoration, and thank Him for suffering so much for you. Beg Him to give you the grace never to offend Him again.

13. Learn the following hymns,
"Pange Lingua"
"Parce Domine"

CHAPTER 18
Living With Christ at Easter and After

> *"He is risen! He is not here!"*
> *"This is the day the Lord hath made;*
> *let us be glad and rejoice therein.*
> *Alleluia."*

Do you know why the Church uses these very joyful words on Easter Sunday and during the Easter Season? Are you ready to celebrate the glorious feast of Easter? You spent Holy Week suffering with Christ, and finished the beautiful liturgy of Holy Saturday with the Mass of the Resurrection. Happiness overflows as you rejoice with Christ and His Church in His great victory over sin and death. Now that Satan and sin are conquered, supernatural life and eternal happiness can be yours.

Easter is the greatest feast of the Church year. It is of great importance in our life.

The Easter season, though most essentially about Jesus' victory over death, can be understood in terms of a threefold resurrection. The first is in nature. Each year nature awakens from the winter sleep. The ice and snow in the fields and forest are melted by spring's warm winds, and buds appear on trees and bushes. Nature comes to life again. It is God's picture book. Just as God brings back life in nature, so He will restore us to supernatural life if we have sinned.

The second resurrection is Christ's. By His resurrection He finished His great work of our redemption. He triumphed over Satan; by rising from the dead, He gained for us the power to rise

from spiritual death. He becomes the glorified Head of His Mystical Body. Just as spring makes new life in nature, so Easter makes new life in the Church.

The third resurrection is that of divine life in us, who are members of the Mystical Body. We rise to a new life of grace and holiness. The Light has conquered darkness. Life has conquered death. Goodness has conquered sin and evil.

The Church calls this feast the "Solemnity of solemnities" or the "Feast of feasts." In the Divine Office we read: "This day is a holy day of the Lord's own choosing; greet this day with rejoicing, greet this day with triumph!" Do you know why? Easter is the greatest of all feasts because Christ arose from the dead by His own power and proved that He is God. The resurrection of Christ is the foundation of our faith: as Paul tells us, "...if Christ has not been raised, then our proclamation has been in vain and your faith has been in vain." (1 Cor. 15:14).

Easter is the feast of greatest joy. Christ's resurrection is the promise of our future resurrection. The joy is expressed in the Church's liturgy by the frequent repetition of the "Alleluia." "Alleluia" was the great shout of joy of the Israelites of old.

What should be our thoughts on this wonderful feast of Easter? We should recall our own baptism, when we received the divine life. In baptism we arose from sin to the life of grace. We should think about the many times we received the Holy Eucharist, when Christ came to nourish the supernatural life within us. Lastly, we should think of our Confirmation, by which we have been or will be united more closely with Christ in His Mystical Body, the Church. Easter should make us want to re-live the glorious life of Christ triumphant through this feast.

Easter Sunday of the Resurrection of the Lord

(Beginning of Easter Week)

"I arose and am still with thee, Alleluia." Do you recall the story of the resurrection of Jesus? It is given to us very beautifully in the Mass for Easter Sunday. The liturgy of this day constantly brings to our minds the great truth— "He is risen!" This is the real cause for our rejoicing, for praising and glorifying our Risen Savior. He has truly redeemed us, and we are grateful for this wonderful gift.

How can we show our gratitude to Jesus?

As we move on, re-living the glorious resurrection of Jesus, the Mass tells of Christ's great victory over death and sin. It reminds us of our death to sin through Baptism and of our new life of grace in Christ.

St. Paul speaks to us in the Epistle, and asks us to purify our hearts of sins and faults which displease God and to receive the glorious Christ with a pure heart.

In the Gospel, St. Mark relates the inspiring story of the holy women going to the tomb to anoint the body of Jesus. Do you remember what happened when they reached the sepulcher? An angel told them that Jesus was not there, that He had risen, and that He would meet His disciples in Galilee. See how thoughtful Jesus was of His friends! The holy women spread the good news of Christ's resurrection. You can be like them when you lead others to Christ by your actions and words. By acting like Christ you can bring others to Him. Sometimes our little acts of kindness and obedience are just the means to help others find Christ. They see Him in us.

We continue to celebrate the glorious resurrection of Christ as we join with the priest in offering the Holy Sacrifice of the Mass to the heavenly Father in gratitude for our redemption. We rejoice with Christ, our Head, who paid the debt of sin in our stead and who rose glorious from the dead. We ask Him to overcome sin in our hearts and to make us strong with His divine life.

On certain occasions a special hymn is added after the readings. This hymn is called a Sequence. It pays special honor to Christ, or to the Holy Spirit, or to the Holy Eucharist. Easter time is one of these special occasions. The Sequence "Victimae Paschali" ("To the Paschal Victim," i.e., to Christ) is sung on Easter Sunday and throughout the eight days that follow. Join Holy Mother Church as she asks all of us to join and rejoice with the victorious Christ.

"Jesus loves hidden souls. A hidden flower is the most fragrant. I must strive to make the interior of my soul a resting place for the Heart of Jesus."

—St. Faustina Kowalska

Many times the liturgy of Easter Week brings to our attention the Risen Savior appearing to His Apostles and friends after His resurrection. Christ came to strengthen their faith and ours, and to bring us the joy of salvation.

Second Sunday of Easter (Divine Mercy Sunday)

Traditionally, the first Sunday after Easter was called "Low Sunday," because it is of a lower rank than Easter Sunday. In the year 2000, shortly after the canonization of St. Maria Faustina, it was decreed by the Church that the Second Sunday of Easter would be called "Divine Mercy Sunday." The theme of mercy was largely inspired by the remarkable private revelations of St. Maria Faustina, combined with the Church's ever-present desire to emphasize an essential Christian reality: the perfect mercy offered now to all of us through Christ's death and resurrection. On this day, all Catholics around the world are asked to meditate on the mercy of Jesus Christ. Indeed, we are encouraged to receive this mercy through the sacraments of the Church, especially though Penance and Reconciliation and the Eucharist. Pope St. John Paul II strongly encouraged the faithful to develop a devotion to the merciful heart of Jesus, particularly as articulated by St. Faustina in her Diary. Have you ever heard of the Chaplet of Divine Mercy? This chaplet comes to us from the diary of St. Faustina. In addition to the frequent reception of the sacraments, praying the Divine Mercy Chaplet, particularly at the three o'clock hour (in commemoration of Christ's death), can assist our devotion to the merciful heart of Jesus.

The Liturgy of the Word for Divine Mercy Sunday will include passages that focus on the theme of mercy and forgiveness. From the Gospel, you may hear the account of doubting Thomas, who insisted upon touching the wounds of Christ before believing in our Lord's resurrection. Depending on what cycle you are in (A, B, or C) you may alternatively hear the Parable of the Prodigal Son: upon the return of his lost son, the father calls upon his whole household to celebrate and rejoice, for his son was "was dead and is come to life again; he was lost, and is found" (Lk. 15:32). We are all prodigal sons, and God forgives us and accepts us with unspeakable joy whenever we repent and return to Him. As St. Paul tells us, "For if, when we were enemies, we were reconciled to God by the death of his Son; much more, being reconciled, shall we be saved by his life" (Rom. 5:10). Perhaps nothing speaks more of God's mercy than that while we were still enemies of God, God loved us and reconciled us to Himself through Jesus Christ. It is no wonder that Pope St. John Paul II referred to God's loving mercy as His greatest attribute and perfection. How fitting it is that we celebrate His mercy every Second Sunday of Easter.

The Easter Season (Continued)

When someone saves another's life, we find the story in the news. We read the whole account to discover when, where, and how a person risked his life in order to save another from death. And this is what Christ has done for us. He gave His life to save us from supernatural death. During the Easter season the Church has us meditate on various aspects of Christ's saving work.

The Road to Emmaus

During this Easter season, we are reminded of the story of the Road to Emmaus, where Jesus meets two disciples on their way. Amidst their doubt and confusion regarding the events that have come to pass, Jesus opens the Scriptures to them, but their eyes are kept from recognizing Him. After hearing Jesus speak on the

Scriptures, the disciples invite Him into their home. He stays the evening, and breaks bread in their midst: "And their eyes were opened, and they knew him: and he vanished out of their sight. And they said one to the other: Was not our heart burning within us, whilst he spoke in this way, and opened to us the scriptures?'" (Lk. 24:31–32). Do you recognize a pattern in this story? Does it remind you of something Catholics partake of? The Road to Emmaus, in many ways, is like the Mass we experience today. The Scriptures are opened up to us, and after receiving God's word, we partake in the Bread of Life. Christ continues His saving work through His Word, and through the Eucharist.

The Good Shepherd

Christ is the Good Shepherd—we will hear this message during the Easter season as well. While we are still thinking of Easter and its wonderful spirit of peace, joy, and faith, we are reminded of our Risen Christ, the Good Shepherd who lays down His life for us His sheep: "I am the good shepherd; and I know mine, and mine know me. As the Father knows me, and I know the Father: and I lay down my life for my sheep" (John 10:14–15).

Perhaps an explanation about the work of a shepherd may help us understand why Christ said that His Church is like a sheepfold.

The sheepfold is usually a large field with a high wall or fence built around it. At night the sheep are gathered into it. A guard is left at the gate or door to keep the night watch. Early in the morning the chief shepherd enters by the door and calls his sheep, who know his voice and begin to move forward toward the gate. The rams, being the leaders, go out first; then all the other sheep follow. Once out in the open, they follow the lead of their shepherd because they know his voice. The shepherd leads the sheep to good pastures and refreshing waters. The sheep know that they are in good hands and that their master will protect them with his life.

How does this help us to understand Christ, our Good Shepherd? Another good shepherd of souls tells us, St. Peter, who was the first one to take Christ's place as shepherd in the Church. What does he tell us? First of all, he reminds us that Christ, the Son of God, became our Good Shepherd and gave His life for our salvation. He also tells us that Jesus left us an example that we should follow (1 Peter 2). Can you name some of the things Christ did that we could imitate? St. Peter also reminds us that when we sin we are like stray sheep, but that we can return to Christ's sheepfold by sorrow and confession. It is then that Christ can say to us and of us: "I am the good shepherd, and I know mine and mine know me" (Jn. 10:14).

The Gospel of St. John relates the touching story of the Good Shepherd. Here Christ Himself tells us what He thinks of us. He tries to make us realize how precious we are in His sight. As a Good Shepherd He gave His life for us, and in the Holy Eucharist He continues to give us His life. If we have had the misfortune to fall by the wayside into sinful ways, by the grace of His sacraments He seeks, finds, and takes us back into the safety of His sheepfold. Does the Good Shepherd ask us to do anything for Him? Yes indeed. He wants us to bring other sheep into the Sheepfold, the Catholic Church. Are you doing anything to win other sheep for Christ—at least by prayer and good example?

How does Christ take care of His sheepfold? Do you recall what He said before He suffered and died for us? He told us that He would never leave us orphans. He kept His promise! First of all, He remains with us in the Most Holy Sacrament of the altar—to be our strength, our food, and our life. Second, He appointed St. Peter and his successors to take His place in ruling the Church, which is the reason why we call the Holy Father Christ's Vicar on earth. He has charge of all Christ's sheep, and is interested even in those who are not as yet members of His flock. Next we have the Holy Father's helpers, the bishops, who care for the members of Christ's Mystical Body in areas we know as dioceses; then there are the pastors, who guide Christ's sheep in smaller units known as parishes; and last, there are the priests who assist pastors in carrying out their work. Do you see how well Christ takes care of His own? We are His; we belong to Him and He cares for us with a loving Father's care. What is our part in this plan? We must try to be good sheep of the Good Shepherd and do everything we can, especially by prayer and good example, to draw "other sheep" into Christ's fold.

> "I am the good shepherd, and I know mine and mine know me" (Jn. 10:14).

"O Death, where is your sting? O Hell, where is your victory? Christ is risen, and you are overthrown. Christ is risen, and the demons are fallen. Christ is risen, and the angels rejoice. Christ is risen, and life reigns. Christ is risen, and not one dead remains in the grave. For Christ, being risen from the dead, is become the first fruits of those who have fallen asleep. To Him be glory and dominion unto ages of ages."

ST. JOHN CHRYSOSTOM

The Risen Christ

Since Easter Sunday, the liturgy of the Church has directed our whole attention to the Risen Christ. On the Sundays following Easter Sunday, Christ's Mystical Body the Church will celebrate not only the Resurrection, but also the whole mystery of the Redemption. Let us recall Christ's words to His Apostles, "A little while and you shall see me no longer; and again a little while and you shall see me, because I go to the Father" (Jn. 16:16).

Have you ever thought of Christ as a prisoner? He has made Himself an Exile for love of us. He became man to save us. After He had finished the work that the Father had given Him, it was time for Christ to return to His heavenly Father. How do you suppose He felt? Christ had a great longing to go home, but somehow His strong desires were overshadowed by His concern for us.

When Christ spoke of going "home" to His heavenly Father, He comforted His Apostles by telling them that in leaving them He was going to prepare a place for them in heaven. His thoughts were always directed toward us. Christ said that in a little while they shall no longer see Him, and again in a little while they shall see Him. That sounds like a riddle, does it not? What did Jesus mean by the "little while"? Christ tried to make His Apostles and us understand that this earth is not our real home; that our life here is short when compared with eternity. When we die we shall not only see Jesus, but we shall make our home with Him. Life is short, heaven is our true home.

St. Peter describes Christians as "pilgrims and strangers" on earth (1 Peter 2:11). We are here only for a while. Our aim is to reach the place which Christ prepared for us in heaven. What must we do to reach our eternal home? St. Peter encourages us to follow closely in the footsteps of the gloriously Risen Savior by imitating Him. How can we imitate Jesus? Christ instructs us to love our neighbors and our enemies, to show special love to the members of the Mystical Body of Christ, to have great reverence toward God, and to obey our lawful superiors. And above all, Christ wants us to carry our crosses for love of Him.

If we do this we are walking in the footsteps of our Lord. We may then be sure that He will help us reach our true home. Then too, others seeing us can see and find Christ.

Hope of a Helper

Christ must ascend to heaven if His work for men is to continue. In the Gospel we hear Christ repeat again and again that He must leave the world and go to His heavenly Father. "But I speak the truth to you; it is expedient for you that I depart. For if I do not go, the Advocate will not come to you; but if I go, I will send him to you" (Jn. 16:7–8). The "Advocate" or Helper is the Holy Spirit, the Third Person of the Blessed Trinity. Once Christ, the Second Person of the Blessed Trinity, had finished His work of Redemption, the Holy Spirit would come to sanctify this work and bring its blessings to men of all times.

Do we realize why Christ made these truths so clear and strong? He wanted to prepare us in a very special manner for the coming of the Spirit of truth and love. He knew that by returning to His heavenly Father He could send the Holy Spirit to us, so that He could teach us all truth and be our guide to holiness.

To reach the home Christ has prepared for us in heaven, we must work with the Holy Spirit. Sanctifying grace, which Christ merited for us on Calvary, is a precious gift. Through it we become friends of God and heirs to heaven. This grace is kept alive in us by the Holy Spirit. But He will not make us holy unless we work with many actual graces He sends to help us in our daily life. We must realize how much we need His help and we must do all we can to co-operate with the Holy Spirit in this great work of becoming saints.

The Work of Christ in the World

The end of the Easter season is fast approaching, and we are again invited to celebrate the glorious mysteries of the Risen Savior. We rejoice with Christ because by His victory He delivered us from eternal death. Christ tells us that all we need to do is ask Him for help, and He will help us. The best way of asking in Christ's name is by praying with the Church. What better prayer do we have than the Mass, and the Divine Office, the perfect prayer of Christ's Mystical Body?

Jesus makes the solemn promise that if we ask for anything in His name, God will grant it to us. "Amen, amen, I say to you, if you ask the Father anything in my name, he will give it to you" (Jn. 16:23). Christ teaches us how to pray, how to ask for the graces we need to gain heaven. He encourages us to pray with childlike trust and confidence, promising us that God will hear and answer our prayers. God knows what is best for us, and that is what He gives us.

Christ tells us: "I came forth from the Father and have come into the world. Again I leave the world and go to the Father" (Jn. 16:28). This reminds us of the two divisions of the Church Year. "I came forth from the Father and have come into the world." This is the Christmas season. "Again I leave the world and go to the Father." This refers to the Easter season.

Christ came to earth to carry out His Father's will. We, too, are here on earth to do God's will by living according to the pattern Christ gives us in the liturgy—in our work, prayers, and play. All the things we have studied about this year should help us "be doers of the word, and not hearers only" (James 1:22).

The Ascension of the Lord

"He ascended into heaven, and is seated at the right hand of the Father." As we pray this article of the Creed, we think of all the things that happened during the forty days that Christ remained on earth after His Resurrection. During this time Christ showed His Apostles that He had truly risen from the dead and that He was, therefore, God. Second, Christ had to make His Apostles understand that the kingdom He came to establish was not an earthly kingdom but a spiritual one. Third, He had to give them advice on how to care for the Kingdom He had founded, the Catholic Church. The Apostles were to play an important role in this great work. Theirs was a special vocation to be shepherds of Christ's sheep.

How did Jesus do all this work? During the forty days after His resurrection He often spoke of His kingdom on earth and of the need of His going away, so that the Holy Spirit could come and help the Apostles realize their vocation. From the liturgy of the Sundays after Easter we have learned how Christ taught His Apostles, and gave them powers which would help them to do the work entrusted to them. Thus, day after day, Christ taught, helped, and guided His Apostles. Then came the day when Christ said that He must leave them; that unless He returned to His heavenly Father, the Holy Spirit would not come to them. The hearts of the Apostles grew sad, but again Christ consoled them. He told them that when the Holy Spirit would come He would teach them all things that they should need to know.

Once more Christ was in the Supper Room where He had given us the gift of Himself in the Holy Eucharist. After His farewell talk to those whom He loved most, He slowly took them along the path that led to the top of the Mount of Olives. Of what was He thinking? What was in their minds? Once again, they crossed the valley, the Brook of Cedron, and continued walking up the

Mount of Olives. What memories filled His heart as He thought of His bloody sweat, His capture, and the desertion of His Apostles! The foot of this little mount saw the greatest humiliation of His life, and now its top was to see the beginning of His great glory. Christ willed to begin His Passion on the lower slopes of Mount Olivet, and it was also His will that He begin His reign of glory by ascending to heaven from its summit.

As the beloved Master raised His hand in blessing, He was seen to rise from the ground and ascend into heaven. What does this mystery mean? It means that Christ, our brother, ascended into heaven, body and soul, to take possession of the reward He merited by His obedience to the will of His heavenly Father. In this mystery it is Christ's humanity that was glorified. As God, Christ was never separated from His Father. Did He not say very often: "I and the Father are one"? But Christ as the God-Man merited the glory of sitting at the right hand of the Father because He fulfilled God's holy will in its smallest detail. This obedience was particularly shown in His passion and death. As Christ told His disciples after His Resurrection "Did not the Christ have to suffer these things before entering into his glory?" (Lk. 24:26.)

Both the Mass and the Divine Office present over and over again the beautiful picture of Christ's Ascension into heaven. "Men of Galilee, why do you stand looking up to heaven? . . . [He] will come in the same way as you have seen him going up to heaven" (Acts 1:11). "They saw him lifted up, and a cloud caught him up into heaven, alleluia" (Vesper Antiphon).

The prayers during Mass remind us that we should live holy lives, thinking about heavenly things, because Christ our Lord and Savior is in heaven. Through the readings of the Mass we have a chance to spend time with Jesus during His last hours on earth.

As we think about this wonderful mystery of the Ascension of Christ into heaven, what should be our thoughts? We know that Christ, in order to send us the Holy Spirit, went to prepare a place for us. We know that the Holy Spirit is the life-giving Spirit, the One who brings us supernatural life and makes us holy. We can be sure of securing our place in heaven by co-operating with the graces which the Holy Spirit comes to give us. Sin is the chain that keeps us bound to earth. We must break the chain by giving up sin though repentance, reconciliation, and the power of the Holy Spirit.

FOR ME TO REVIEW

Catechism Lesson

93. **Q. What do you mean by saying that Christ sits at the right hand of God the Father?**

A. When I say that Christ sits at the right hand of God the Father I mean that Christ as God is equal to His Father in all things, and that as man He is in the highest place in heaven next to God.

408. **Q. When will Christ judge us?**
A. Christ will judge us immediately after our death, and on the last day.

409. **Q. What is the judgment called which we have to undergo immediately after death?**
A. The judgment we have to undergo immediately after death is called the particular judgment.

410. **Q. What is the judgment called which all men have to undergo on the last day?**
A. The judgment which all men have to undergo on the last day is called the general judgment.

Questions

Match the words in Column A with the sentences in Column B.

Column A	**Column B**
A. Easter	1. The appearances of Jesus strengthened this virtue in the Apostles.
B. Holy Spirit	2. Christ arose from the dead.
C. Divinity	3. Lifting up of our hearts and minds to God.
D. Passion and Death	4. The resurrection of Christ was proof of this.
E. Victory	5. By these means Christ earned grace for mankind.
F. Faith	6. Jesus went back to His heavenly Father.
G. Sequence	7. The hymn sung after the Gradual of the Mass on Easter and during the octave.
H. Ascension	8. Another word for triumph.
I. Prayer	9. Our Teacher and Guide whom Christ sent us.

FOR ME TO REMEMBER

1. Easter is the great feast of Christ's Resurrection from the dead.
2. The resurrection of Christ is a proof of His divinity.
3. The resurrection of Christ is a promise of our future resurrection.
4. Christ our Redeemer triumphed over sin and death.
5. The Spirit of Easter is one of joy and peace, faith and hope.
6. The Sundays after Easter direct our hearts and minds heavenward because during this time Christ often told His Apostles about heaven.
7. Christ appeared to His Apostles and disciples to strengthen their faith in His divinity.
8. Christ ascended into heaven to receive the glory which He merited by His life, Passion, and death.
9. Christ promised to send us the Holy Spirit who would be our teacher and guide.
10. Christ ascended into heaven forty days after His Resurrection.

FOR ME TO DO

1. List some of the things you like about the Easter Liturgy. Discuss them.
2. Find passages in the New Testament to show:
   that the Apostles received power from Christ to forgive sins.
   that the Apostles were told to preach the Gospel to all nations.
   a proof that there are three persons in one God.
   that Christ will reward us for believing in Him.
3. Explain the difference between a shepherd and a hireling (as explained by the Parable of the Good Shepherd).

4. Compose an original prayer to our Risen Lord to thank Him for the gift of Redemption.
6. Relate some of our Lord's appearances and tell why they are meaningful.
7. Which Sequence is said during Easter Week, and whom does it praise?
8. Explain the truth that the current pope is the successor of St. Peter.
9. Explain the Easter Season of the Liturgical Year.
10. Choose an important world leader and pray for him often so that he may do what God wants him to do.

Summary of Unit 5

The Easter Season is the second part of the great drama of our redemption. It is preceded by a season of preparation, Lent; followed by a season of application, Pentecost. During Lent we join Christ, our Head, in His sufferings. We unite our own sacrifices to His in order to atone for our sins and to win new members for His Mystical Body.

On Palm Sunday we enter Jerusalem with Christ in triumph. On Holy Thursday night we are with the Apostles, when Christ instituted the Holy Eucharist.

On Good Friday we join the Blessed Virgin at the foot of the cross, sorrowing over our sins which alone caused Christ's death.

On Holy Saturday we renew our baptismal vows to prepare for Easter, the most glorious feast of the Liturgical Year. With our hearts renewed, we glory with Him on Easter, the day commemorating His glorious resurrection.

On the Sundays after Easter, up until the Ascension, we think of heavenly things, longing for the day when we shall be reunited to Christ in His heavenly home.

Write your answers on a separate sheet of paper

Part 1 Multiple Choice

Write the choice that best completes the sentence.

1. In the gospel story about the master and the vineyard, the promised pay given to the workers reminds us of:
   A. a reward on earth.
   B. our allowances.
   C. the reward of heaven.
   D. change mother gives us.
2. The Easter season lasts from the first Sunday of Lent until:
   A. Pentecost.
   B. Trinity Sunday.
   C. Easter.
   D. the Ascension.
3. We rejoice on the middle Sunday of Lent, Laetare Sunday, because:
   A. we are tired of Lent.
   B. Easter is almost here.
   C. we get our throats blessed.
   D. there are flowers on the altar.
4. The Church wishes to draw our attention to the great sufferings and the coming death of Christ especially during:
   A. Lent.
   B. the feast of the Transfiguration.
   C. Christmas Season.
   D. Easter.

5. Christ, the Son of God, in His Passion and death, hid His divinity from the world. The Church shows this in her liturgy from Palm Sunday to Holy Saturday by:
   A. asking us to say more rosaries.
   B. covering the statues and crucifixes from view.
   C. hoping we do not look at TV.
   D. reading the Passion to us.
6. The Paschal Candle is a symbol of:
   A. the Passion.
   B. Christ, Light of the World.
   C. the Presentation.
   D. the Blessed Mother.
7. Easter is the greatest of all feasts because:
   A. we wear new clothes.
   B. the altars are decorated with lilies.
   C. we eat chocolate Easter eggs.
   D. Christ conquered death through His resurrection and in doing so atoned for our sin.
8. The glorious Easter liturgy constantly reminds us of this great truth:
   A. Christ suffered for our sins.
   B. Christ will soon go up into heaven.
   C. Christ is risen.
   D. Christ lived on earth.
9. If we are to be loving, faithful children of Jesus Christ, it is not enough for us merely to keep from sin. We must love and live as Christ did by:
   A. praying often.
   B. honoring our parents.
   C. doing acts of charity.
   D. all of the above.

Part 2 True-False

Mark each statement T if it is True and F if it is False.

1. A temptation is a sin.
2. To abstain means to keep from doing or using.
3. Mary shows us what living with Christ means.
4. From the sufferings and death of Christ we learn God's love for man and the evil of sin.
5. God allows us to be tempted to test and refine our faith.
6. The resurrection of Christ was a proof that He was man.
7. Traditionally, and in the extraordinary from, Easter season includes a pre-Lenten period.
8. Christ's resurrection is a promise of our future resurrection.

Part 3 Arrange in Order

Arrange these in correct order according to their proper place in the Liturgical Year.

A. Palm Sunday
B. Holy Saturday
C. Laetare Sunday
D. Holy Thursday
E. Ascension Thursday
F. Good Friday
G. Ash Wednesday
H. Easter

Regina Caeli

Queen of Heaven, rejoice, alleluia.
For he, whom you did merit to bear, alleluia.
Has risen as he said, alleluia.
Pray for us to God, alleluia.

V. Rejoice and be glad, O Virgin Mary, alleluia.
R. For the Lord is truly risen, alleluia.

Let us pray: O God, who gave joy to the world through the resurrection of thy Son, our Lord Jesus Christ, grant we beseech thee, that through the intercession of the Virgin Mary, his Mother, we may obtain the joys of everlasting life. Through the same Christ our Lord. Amen.

UNIT

6 Living With Christ in His Church—Pentecost to Advent

From Pentecost until Advent we live with the Third Person of God, the Holy Spirit, gathering the gifts and fruits of the Redemption as He incorporates us into the Mystical Body of Christ, helping each of us live the life of charity toward God, our neighbor, and ourselves.

During the last part of the Liturgical Year we will learn more about God's love for us. We will learn about His love in sending the Holy Spirit.

The period after Pentecost is the longest of the liturgical seasons. It extends to the beginning of Advent, the time varying depending on whether Easter is early or late. This in between season is called Ordinary Time. Ordinary Time, in the liturgical calendar, refers to any time in the Liturgical Year outside of Christmas (and Advent) or Easter (and Lent). There are thirty-four weeks in Ordinary Time, beginning in January, and ending just before Advent.

As true children of Mother Church we should care for the divine life we received in Baptism by receiving the sacraments frequently, by assisting at the Holy Sacrifice of the Mass, by prayer, and by good works. In this way only can we prepare ourselves for the time when Christ will come again as Judge of the living and the dead.

The readings for Ordinary Time call our attention to Christ's teachings and His miracles. They tell us how Christ healed the sick, comforted the sorrowing, and raised the dead. In this way He taught the lessons of love and charity. They are also guides to help us lead a good Christian life, and thus become more Christlike in all our daily actions.

CHAPTER 19

Living With the Holy Spirit as Members of the Mystical Body of Christ

Vigil of Pentecost

As with every other great feast, Pentecost has a vigil, a day to cleanse ourselves and prepare for the great holy day.

In the early days of the Church solemn baptism was administered on the Vigil of Pentecost to those who could not receive it at Easter time. The Vigil of Pentecost is a good time to think of our own baptism. On that day we can again renew our baptismal vows, that with the help and strength of the Holy Spirit we may live united always with Christ.

The liturgy for the Vigil Mass refers to the coming of the Holy Spirit. The Holy Spirit is also called the Paraclete, which means “helper” or “counselor.” Christ promised to send us “a helper” when He spoke to His Apostles at the Last Supper. The entire Mass of Pentecost is one which shows the great longing of the Church for the coming of the Holy Spirit with His spiritual gifts. With Mother Church, we should celebrate Pentecost with joy, with a strong faith and a desire to grow in holiness.

Pentecost

Previously, we reviewed the part of the Apostles' Creed which states: "I believe in the Holy Spirit, the Holy Catholic Church." We also learned the answers to these questions:

1. **Who is the Holy Spirit?**
2. **When did the Holy Spirit come down upon the Apostles?**
3. **Why were the Apostles together in the Upper Room?**
4. **What is Baptism?**
5. **What is Confirmation?**

Do you remember them?

Now we come to that very special feast which recalls the day on which our Blessed Lord sent the Holy Spirit upon the Apostles and founded the Church. Pentecost means "fiftieth," which originally signified the Jewish festival occurring fifty days after the Passover. As the book of Acts tells us, it was to celebrate this very festival that the disciples, and many other Jews from far and wide, were gathered together in Jerusalem. What happened that day among the apostles is the basis for the distinctly Christian meaning of Pentecost, which—just like the Jewish festival—occurs fifty days after Easter.

> "On the day of Pentecost when the seven weeks of Easter had come to an end, Christ's Passover is fulfilled in the outpouring of the Holy Spirit, manifested, given, and communicated as a divine person: of his fullness, Christ, the Lord, pours out the Spirit in abundance."
>
> —*Catechism of the Catholic Church*, 731

Traditionally, the Feast of Pentecost was also called Whitsunday (meaning "White Sunday"), which derives from the practice in the early centuries of giving solemn baptism on the vigil of that day. Those who were baptized wore their white robes at the Pentecost Mass.

Pentecost marks the birthday of the Church because the descent of the Holy Spirit fully prepared the Church for her mission on earth. So powerfully did the Holy Spirit begin to carry out His work on that day that in Jerusalem itself three thousand persons came to belief in Christ and were baptized. This was the beginning of the victory march of the Church which no evil person or government has ever been able to stop, or will ever *be able* to stop, for Christ promised, "the gates of hell shall not prevail against it" (Mt. 16:18).

The Holy Spirit came down upon the Apostles in "a mighty rush of wind" and in the form of "parted tongues as of fire" (Acts 2:3). We, too, should ask for grace like that which Christ sent His Apostles, grace which burns out everything sinful in us. Unlike physical fire, we should not be afraid of the heat of God's flame of love. Though it may cause a certain purifying pain, the pain will go away and leave us pure and clean. Often repeat the following: "Come, Holy Spirit, fill the hearts of thy faithful and kindle in them the fire of Thy divine love. Send forth Thy spirit and they shall be created, and Thou shalt renew the face of the earth."

The Holy Spirit did not leave the Church after the Apostles died; He remains with Christ's Mystical Body forever. He is the giver of all gifts, the light of every mind, the joy of every heart. Without Him there is nothing good in man. He washes away our sins, sends down grace, and heals our wounds. He warms our cold hearts and guides our wandering feet. He is the giver of the life of grace! He is the giver of eternal joy! Just as we pray to the Father, and the Son, we should never forget to pray to the Holy Spirit!

It was through the Holy Spirit that Mary became the Mother of God. This same Spirit guided Christ in His earthly life as Jesus said, "The Spirit of the Lord is upon me" (Lk. 4:18).

The distribution of the graces of redemption also is the work of the Holy Spirit. This work is still carried on in the Church, especially in the Mass and in the sacraments.

The same Holy Spirit comes to us in Baptism and Confirmation. We, too, are filled with the power from on high. The Third Person of the Blessed Trinity is continually at work in the sacraments, blessings, and liturgy of the Church, making us holy. The Holy Spirit dwells in us until driven out by mortal sin. What holy lives would we live if we always remembered that the Holy Spirit lives within us!

When Peter preached his first sermon to the people of Jerusalem that first Pentecost Sunday, they asked: "What shall we do?" Your priests, teachers, and parents often speak to you about God and the teachings of the Church. You must not only listen, you must also do what is rightly asked of you.

Try to be very attentive during your lessons on the Catholic faith, and see how many things you can do to be a Christ-like boy or girl. Here is a small guide on how to act in accordance with our Catholic faith:

1. I know that God is present on the altar. I will show that I know it by my good behavior at Mass.
2. I know that God sees and knows all things. I will remember that when I am tempted to cheat or do wrong, whether I am at school or anywhere else.
3. I know that God has commanded me to love and obey my parents. I will show today that I am obeying this commandment by cheerfully doing all that they ask me.
4. I know I am commanded never to steal. I will show that I wish to obey God's seventh commandment by removing myself from whatever situations lead me into temptation.
5. I know I am a temple of the Holy Spirit. I will show that I know this by avoiding everything that is impure.

Meditating on the first Pentecost reminds us of the continuing work of Christ in the Church through the Person of the Holy Spirit, whom He promised to send: "I will not leave you orphans" (Jn. 14:18).Like the Apostles, we are to become changed members of the Mystical Body of Christ. We are to be filled with eager desire and love for the things of the kingdom of Christ.

Like Easter Week, Pentecost is a time of joy. Each day has its special Mass to tell of the workings of the Holy Spirit in the world, in the Church, and in men. The color of the vestments for the Mass is red, which is the color of fire and love.

The Most Holy Trinity

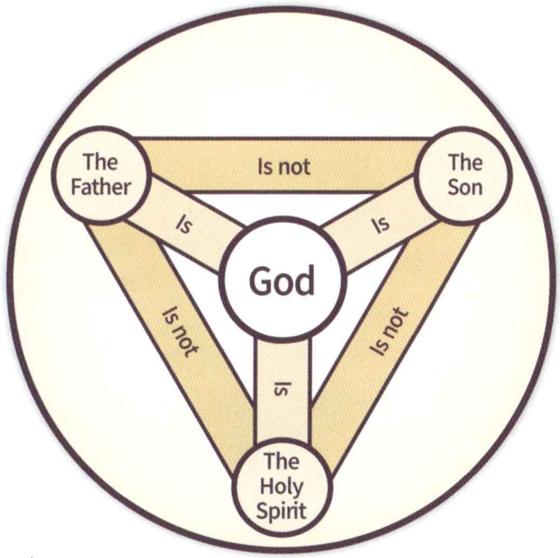

Shield of the Trinity or *Scutum Fidei,* used throughout history to illustrate the Blessed Trinity

On the solemnity of the Most Holy Trinity, we stop to look at the basic things we believe: we recall the mysteries of Christmas, when God the Father sent His divine Son into the world; of Easter, when the divine Son redeemed mankind by His death and glorious resurrection; and of Pentecost, when the Holy Spirit came to sanctify us. We see here the infinite love of the three divine Persons for each of us, and we join with Christ and His Mystical Body, the Church, in thanking and loving God for it.

The work of the Blessed Trinity began in us when we were baptized in the name of the three Divine Persons. In each sacrament which we receive, the Blessed Trinity continues this work—for every sacrament is administered in the name of the Father, and of the Son, and of the Holy Spirit.

We often make the sign of the cross, say the beautiful prayer "Glory be to the Father, and to the Son and to the Holy Spirit," recite the Creed, and assist at Holy Mass. Whenever we do this, we express our belief in the three divine Persons and give honor to the Father who created us, the Son who redeemed us, and the Holy Spirit who sanctified us. Do we begin and close each day by reverently making the sign of the cross thus blessing ourselves in the name of the Father, and of the Son, and of the Holy Spirit?

In the letter to the Romans, St. Paul would have us realize the greatness of this mystery. He cries out, "Oh, the depth of the riches of the wisdom and of the knowledge of God! How incomprehensible are his judgments and how unsearchable his ways! . . . from him and through him and unto him are all things" (Rom. 11:33, 36). We will never be able to understand how good, how wise, and all-knowing God is! Do we show by our conduct that we appreciate the wonderful things that God the Father, God the Son, and God the Holy Spirit have done for us?

In the Gospel of Matthew, we hear that Jesus Christ founded His Church on the Apostles: "Go, therefore, and make disciples of all nations" (Mt. 28:19). Thank God for the wonderful gift of being a member of His Mystical Body, the Church, in which His divine life becomes the beginning of our supernatural life.

In gratitude for the great love God has shown to each of us, repeat the prayer of the Mass for the Feast of the Most Holy Trinity: "Blessed be God the Father, and the only-begotten Son of God, and also the Holy Spirit because He has shown His mercy to us."

The Most Holy Body and Blood of Christ (Corpus Christi)

After the important feasts of the Holy Spirit and the Most Holy Trinity, the Church returns to Christ, celebrating the feasts of Corpus Christi, the Sacred Heart, and the Immaculate Heart.

The Feast of Corpus Christi is a solemn act of faith in the Real Presence of Jesus Christ in the Blessed Eucharist. On this feast we celebrate the goodness of our Lord in leaving us His Body and Blood to be our food and drink. In the Gospel of John, Christ tells us: "He who eats my flesh, and drinks my blood, abides in me and *I* in him" (Jn. 6:57).

We know that Christ instituted the Holy Eucharist at the Last Supper on Holy Thursday. The Church reminds us of this wonderful gift during the Mass for that day. Do you remember the beautifully decorated altar, the glad music of the organ, and the joyful ringing of the bells at the Gloria—and then the silence? Just for a short time the Church put aside the sorrows and mourning of Holy Week to celebrate the institution of the Blessed Sacrament. To honor Christ in the Eucharist the Church also has the feast of *Corpus Christi.*

In the thirteenth century, St. Thomas Aquinas composed a beautiful liturgy for the Feast of Corpus Christi which included some hymns that we still sing today. This man, one of the most brilliant men of all times, was known for his great devotion to the

Blessed Sacrament. His beautiful prayers and hymns draw our attention to the institution of the Holy Eucharist. Christ instituted the Holy Eucharist to be the food and drink of our souls, in order that we might always be united with Him and His members.

This feast brings our mind to the mystery of the Holy Eucharist, to consider Christ as priest; Christ as king; Christ who gives spiritual riches to those who eat of Him. The feast also calls our attention to the various figures of the Old Testament which represented the Holy Eucharist: Bread of Heaven, Paschal Lamb, sacrifice of Melchizedek. The following hymn provides a beautiful summary of the whole Eucharistic mystery: "O Sacred banquet, wherein Christ is received, we commemorate His Passion, the soul is filled with grace and a pledge of future glory is given unto us, alleluia."

In many countries (including many parishes in the United States), the Feast of Corpus Christi is marked by solemn public processions of the faithful by which they express their belief in the presence of Christ in the Blessed Sacrament. The priest carries the Blessed Sacrament in a golden monstrance not only around the church, but through the city streets and country lanes so that all may honor Christ as their King and Ruler, as their God and Savior. When the procession is held out of doors, Benediction of the Most Blessed Sacrament is given at four different altars instead of one.

St. Thomas wrote the beautiful hymn we sing at Benediction, the "Tantum Ergo."

> "Down in adoration falling,
> Lo! the sacred Host we hail,
> Lo! o'er ancient forms departing
> Newer rites of grace prevail;
> Faith for all defects supplying,
> Where the feeble senses fail.

To the Everlasting Father,
And the Son Who reigns on high
With the Holy Ghost proceeding
Forth from Each eternally,
Be salvation, honor, blessing,
Might, and endless majesty. Amen."

Solemnity of the Most Sacred Heart of Jesus

Many years ago, at a time when the love of God was growing cold in the hearts of men, Our Lord appeared to St. Margaret Mary Alacoque, a humble Visitation Sister, while she was at prayer. He showed her His Sacred Heart and asked her to spread devotion to it. "Behold," He said, "the Heart which has loved men so much." Our Lord wanted to remind us of His great love for us in order that we might love Him in return.

How often Christ showed His great love for mankind! Perhaps you can recall a few Bible stories which show Christ's love for sinners, for those who were suffering, for those who were sad, and even for little children. Do you remember the story of Mary Magdalen? Christ forgave her all the terrible sins she had committed. Our Blessed Savior loved Mary Magdalen so much that He even appeared to her after He rose from the dead.

In another story we read about the lepers whom Christ cured of their loathsome disease. Why did Christ cure them? For the same reason He cures each of us of the leprosy of sin when in all humility we ask Him to cure us.

Who could have shown greater love for those who grieved and were troubled than our loving Savior! When Christ met the widow who was burying her only son, His heart was filled with sadness. Again Christ showed His love for His children.

Promises from Jesus for those who honor His Sacred Heart

1. I will give them all the graces necessary in their state of life.
2. I will establish peace in their homes.
3. I will comfort them in all their afflictions.
4. I will be their secure refuge during life, and above all, in death.
5. I will bestow abundant blessings upon all their undertakings.
6. Sinners will find in My Heart the source and infinite ocean of mercy.
7. Lukewarm souls shall become fervent.
8. Fervent souls shall quickly mount to high perfection.
9. I will bless every place in which an image of My Heart is exposed and honored.
10. I will give to priests the gift of touching the most hardened hearts.
11. Those who shall promote this devotion shall have their names written in My Heart.
12. I promise you in the excessive mercy of My Heart that My all powerful love will grant to all those who receive Holy Communion on the First Fridays in nine consecutive months the grace of final perseverance; they shall not die in My disgrace, nor without receiving their sacraments. My divine Heart shall be their safe refuge in this last moment.

He brought the widow's son back to life and gave him to his mother.

Christ loved little children, too. One day when Jesus was resting after a hard day's work, some women brought their children to receive His blessing. The disciples did not want these women and their little ones to disturb their Master because He was tired. However, Christ loved each little child and wanted to give each of them His blessing. He said to His disciples, "Let the little children come to me, and do not hinder them, for of such is the kingdom of God" (Lk. 18:16). In just the same way Christ is waiting for each of us to go to Him and ask His blessing on all we do.

We can find many more examples of Christ's love for us. What are we doing in return? How are we showing love for Christ?

The Feast of the Sacred Heart is often called the feast of the love of Jesus. It was started in order that we might make up for the sins of ingratitude which are committed by so many of His creatures, and also to thank Him for the many blessings we have received.

We can show our love and gratitude to the Sacred Heart by assisting at Mass and receiving Holy Communion on the Feast of the Sacred Heart of Jesus and on the first Friday of each month. In addition, we should try to assist at Sacred Heart devotions and recite the Litany of the Sacred Heart as often as possible. Best of all, we can love others as the Sacred Heart of Jesus loves them.

There are many beautiful prayers to the Sacred Heart which we can say very often. In this way we can help to make up for those who do not give honor to the Sacred Heart or who forget to thank Him for all the wonderful things He has done for them.

The liturgy of the Feast of the Sacred Heart presents all the mysteries—joyous, sorrowful, and glorious—of our Lord's life. It points out His great love for man by coming down to earth, by dying on the cross for our salvation, and by remaining on our altars to help us benefit by the merits of His death.

In the Gospel we learn about the unlimited love of Christ. On the cross His heart was opened with a spear, from it flow the waters of forgiveness and the blood which feeds us in the Holy Eucharist. It is truly a fountain of redemption and of love.

Who would not love a God so filled with love for us? Beg the Sacred Heart to fill our hearts with love for Him and all men.

Let us now look at a few of the feasts of the saints and of our Blessed Lady.

Feasts of the Immaculate Heart and the Visitation of the Blessed Virgin Mary

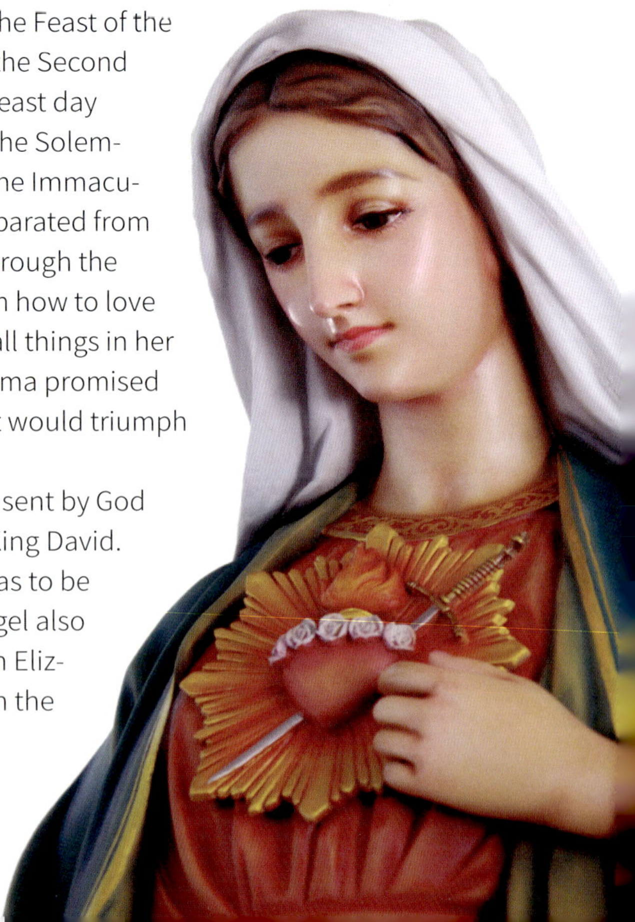

Pope Pius XII established the Feast of the Immaculate Heart during the Second World War. This beautiful feast day occurs the Saturday after the Solemnity of the Sacred Heart. The Immaculate Heart can never be separated from her Son's Sacred Heart. Through the Immaculate Heart we learn how to love Jesus because Mary kept all things in her heart. And our Lady of Fatima promised that her Immaculate Heart would triumph in the end.

The angel Gabriel was sent by God to Mary, a descendant of King David. After telling her that she was to be the mother of God, the angel also announced that her cousin Elizabeth was to have a son. In the feast which shows Mary's response to this news, the liturgy gives us a pattern for our living.

Because Mary was very humble she concealed her own wonderful secret, and thought only of helping Elizabeth, who was very old. She hurried to the hill country to the home of Zachariah. Entering the house she greeted Elizabeth lovingly. When Elizabeth, in her great joy, greeted Mary she exclaimed: "Blessed art thou among women and blessed is the fruit of thy womb" (Lk. 1:42–43). Do you recognize Elizabeth's words? In what prayer are they used?

Mary answered Elizabeth with the beautiful hymn the *Magnificat,* in which she praises the mercy of God, His power, and His fulfillment of the promises to send the Messiah.

> My soul magnifies the Lord.
> And my spirit rejoices in God my Savior.
> Because he has regarded the humility of his handmaid; for behold from henceforth all generations shall call me blessed.
> Because he that is mighty, has done great things to me; and holy is his name.
> And his mercy is from generation unto generations, to them that fear him.
> He has shown might in his arm: he has scattered the proud in the conceit of their heart.
> He has put down the mighty from their seat, and has exalted the humble.
> He has filled the hungry with good things; and the rich he has sent empty away.
> He has received Israel his servant, being mindful of his mercy:
> As he spoke to our fathers, to Abraham and to his seed for ever. (Lk. 1:46–55)

Mary was chosen to be the mother of Christ, the God-Man. We can imagine how kind and helpful she was to Elizabeth and Zachariah. We learn from the Gospel story that Mary, forgetting her own needs, remained with Elizabeth for three months before she returned to her own home in Nazareth. Like Mary, let us carry Christ to all men by being kind and helpful.

> *"In the end, my Immaculate Heart will triumph."*
>
> *—Our Lady of Fatima to the Shepherd Children*

Saints Peter and Paul

The events which are recalled in the feast of the great Apostles Saints Peter and Paul are clearly expressed in the words of the Divine Office:

"This day Simon Peter ascended the agonizing cross, Alleluia. This day the keeper of the keys of heaven went on his way to Christ with joy. This day the Apostle Paul, the light of the world, laying down his life for the name of Christ, was crowned with martyrdom. Alleluia."

St. Peter

Before he was chosen as an Apostle, St. Peter was known as Simon. He and his brother Andrew were fishermen on the shores of the Sea of Galilee. After he became an Apostle, Peter was always treated in a special way by our Lord. He and James and John were permitted to be present during extraordinary events in the life of our Lord. They saw the Transfiguration on Mount Olivet and the agony of Jesus in the Garden. Christ changed Simon's name to Peter or "Rock," and to him He said: ". . . thou art Peter [the Rock], and upon this rock I will build my church" (Mt. 16:18).

Peter was a quick-tempered person, whose tongue often led him into trouble. He even denied Christ three times when Jesus was betrayed. But he was sorry, and never after that was anyone more faithful to the divine Master. After the Resurrection Christ told Peter to "Feed my lambs . . . feed my sheep." Peter was Christ's first vicar on earth, that is, the one who takes His place.

Our Lord made St. Peter the leader of all the Apostles and promised him the help necessary to rule in His name. He told St. Peter that He would protect him, and that He would send the Holy Spirit. He promised that the Holy Spirit would remain with the Church, founded on Peter, for all time. Therefore, whenever St. Peter—or any pope who takes his place—teaches the Church about our Lord's truth, he can never make a mistake. He can never get our Lord's truth wrong, even by accident.

After the Ascension of our Lord, St. Peter governed the Church. He went to Rome, becoming its first bishop. About the

year 67 he died a martyr's death on the cross, with his head downward at his own request. In the place where Peter was buried there arises today the mighty dome of the largest and most beautiful church in Christendom.

St. Paul

Paul was originally known as Saul. He came from the city of Tarsus, in Asia Minor. When he was a young man he was an enemy of the Christians. He helped to find them so they could be put into prison. In fact, he was one of those who worked to have Stephen stoned. He decided to go to Damascus to search for Christians.

As he and his men were riding along the road to Damascus, a big flash of lightning struck him and he was knocked down. Then he heard a voice coming out of the sky, saying "Saul, Saul why do you persecute me?" St. Paul cried out: "Who are you, Lord?" The voice answered: "I am Jesus, whom you are persecuting." St. Paul spoke again and said: "Lord, what will you have me do?" The men who were with him were frightened, for they heard the voice but could not see anyone. They led St. Paul into the city where he stayed for three days fasting. Since he had been knocked

down, he remained blind for three days. On the fourth day a visitor came and said to him: "Brother Saul, the Lord has sent me—Jesus, who appeared to you on your journey—that you may recover your sight and be filled with the Holy Spirit." He could see immediately and he got up and was baptized (Acts 9:1–19).

Paul joined the Christians and preached that "Jesus is the Son of God." The Jews were very angry about Saul and they watched the gates of the city day and night in order to kill him. But the Christians hid him, and one night put him in a basket and lowered him from a window in the wall that was around the city. When he reached the ground on the outside of the wall, St. Paul jumped out of the basket and began a journey at once for Jerusalem.

At Jerusalem the Christians were afraid of Paul, for they did not believe that he was now a Christian. St. Barnabas took Paul to the Apostles and told them how Paul had escaped from Damascus.

The Apostles welcomed St. Paul to join their work for the Church. He made many journeys to many countries. He sailed on the Mediterranean Sea. He started churches wherever he preached. He was always busy. He wrote many letters to the Christian churches explaining Christ's teaching. We call these letters Epistles. There are fourteen letters of St. Paul in the New Testament.

One day, while St. Paul was in Jerusalem, he was arrested and brought to trial. He was in prison a long time, and finally, because he was a Roman citizen, St. Paul appealed to Caesar. So St. Paul was put on board a ship with other prisoners that were sailing for Rome.

When he got to Rome he was kept a prisoner. He stayed there for two years and was beheaded outside the city walls.

Do you know why St. Paul is called the Apostle of the Gentiles? He spent only a short time among the Jewish people because our Lord told him to begin to preach His gospel to all nations.

As soon as he got into a town or city he went about gathering people. That is why he is the first great missionary of the Catholic Church. Then, when he thought that the people knew enough, he would leave them and go away, to bring the gospel to other people.

St. Paul loved Christ so much that he could say: "It is now no longer I that live, but Christ lives in me" (Gal. 2:20). He wanted everyone to live that way, and spent his life showing them how to do it.

For us St. Paul is a wonderful example of the love of Christ. He is a hero, a champion, a martyr, a man we should like to imitate.

On the feast of Saints Peter and Paul the Divine Office presents the main events of the day, namely, the martyrdom of Saints Peter and Paul.

The Gospel of the Mass tells us that when St. Peter received the keys from Christ he became the head of the "kingdom of God on earth"—the Church. It also tells us that Christ gave Peter the power to rule and guide the faithful.

With our holy Mother the Church, we should pray every day for the successor of St. Peter to show our love for the Church, the Catholic faith, and the Holy Father. Do you know the name of the current Holy Father?

Assumption of Our Lady
(August 15)

The Assumption of the Blessed Virgin Mary is one of her great feasts; it is a holy day of obligation. On this day the Church really observes three events. The first of these is Mary's death.

We do not know the time and place of Mary's death. A legend tells how the Apostles returned to her tomb and found fragrant flowers instead of her body. In connection with this legend, in many places on August 15 herbs and flowers are blessed. The

prayer used in the blessing asks for protection of both body and soul from all harmful influences; it also thanks God for the harvest.

Mary's glorious reward for faithful service could be none other than heaven. Mary still lives with us, although she died nearly two thousand years ago. She is loved by more people than any other human person. The liturgy we have studied this year has taught us so many beautiful virtues of our Lady that we do not wonder about the world's great love for her.

The second event celebrated by this feast is the one from which it received its title—The Assumption of our Lady, body and soul, into heaven. The liturgy speaks of our Lady's

"Men do not fear a powerful hostile army as the powers of hell fear the name and protection of Mary."

—St. Bonaventure

entrance into the heavenly kingdom in a great procession of triumph. Can you imagine the arrival of God's Mother in heaven? Can you picture with what tender care and love she was received by her Son and given a special place there? What a glorious welcome the angels must have given their Queen!

The third event is the crowning of Mary as queen of heaven and of all the saints. Our Lady ascended to a place of honor near her divine Son and received the most precious crown of heaven. Here on earth she reached the highest holiness that is possible for anyone. That is why in heaven she has received the greatest honors which can be given to any creature.

The liturgy of this day invites us to unite ourselves with the angels and saints in heaven in their joy and gratitude that the Blessed Virgin was taken, body and soul, into heaven as a reward for her great faith and love. "Thou art the glory of Jerusalem, . . . the joy of Israel."

The Introit says: "A great sign appeared in heaven: a woman clothed with the sun, and the moon was under her feet, and upon her head a crown of twelve stars." The Gospel presents the story of the "Magnificat." "He who is mighty has done great things for me."

In the Divine Office we have the main truths of this great feast summarized and the virtues of our Lady praised. "Mary has been taken up into heaven; the angels rejoice, blessing and praising the Lord." "Virgin most prudent . . . the immaculate Virgin Mary."

We should imitate the virtues of the Blessed Virgin Mary, especially her humility, her life of prayer, and her purity of body and soul. From her childhood, she was so modest that she was the wonder of all. She kept a firm guard over her thoughts, that nothing displeasing ever found an entrance into her mind and heart. God was everything to her and she became the beautiful garden in which He found "great delight."

If we follow the sublime example which Mary gave us we shall one day also be privileged to enter heaven. Remain true to your heavenly Queen and pay tribute to her by frequent recitation of the rosary. She will always remember us, her faithful children.

All Saints' Day (November 1)

Suppose your mother or father or teacher or any other person that you admire very much would let you in on some very special project. They would ask you to help them prepare the materials or arrange for a trip. Wouldn't you be happy, simply thrilled, even though it might mean a great deal of hard work?

Something like this happens in the life of every good Christian boy and girl. Our divine Lord has let us in on His heavenly Father's plan for leading all men to heaven. We on earth can help Christ carry out His plan. The saints in heaven have already done their share. Now they are enjoying God and reigning with Christ the King.

On the Solemnity of All Saints (a holy day of obligation), the Church invites us to picture to ourselves what takes place in heaven on this great feast of the Mystical Body. It also offers some ways and means by which we too can reach eternal life and share in the joys of the saints. The saints in heaven are really our brothers and sisters in Christ, enjoying eternal happiness with Christ their Head.

The Church calls upon us to "rejoice in the Lord as we celebrate the feast in honor of all the saints, upon which the angels rejoice and praise the Son of God."

In the Gospel for this day, our Lord speaks of the Eight Beatitudes. They are our steppingstones to heaven and outline for us a sure way to salvation.

The whole liturgy of the day dwells on the joys and happiness of heaven. In the early morning, Mother Church in her Divine

Office, leads us into heaven and shows us what is going on before the throne of God. "And all the angels that were standing round the throne fell prostrate before the throne and paid God worship." The various hymns praise the numberless classes of saints and angels. We cry out in great surprise: "How glorious is the kingdom wherein all the saints rejoice in Christ; clothed in white robes they are the Lamb's attendants, wherever He goes." Can you tell who is the Lamb?

Ask all the saints to pray that we may better understand God's plan for us. Ask them to aid us to become useful helpers in carrying out this plan. We want to become saints, don't we? It isn't too difficult. Our Lord is willing to help us. The Holy Spirit gives us strength and many graces if we only want to use them. Do you recall when the Holy Spirit came to you for the first time? When did He come the second time? What gifts did He bring to you? These gifts make it much easier for you to follow the teachings of God and live good lives.

All Souls' Day (November 2)

In the Apostles' Creed we say, "I believe in the communion of saints." Do you remember what we mean by the communion of saints? Earlier in our Catechism we learned that by the communion of saints we mean the union of the faithful on earth, the blessed in heaven, and the souls in purgatory with Christ as their Head.

Since we are all one great family in the Catholic Church, we should love and help one another as much as we can, especially in our spiritual needs.

On All Souls' Day we particularly remember the poor souls in purgatory. They are the members of the Mystical Body of Christ who need help desperately. They are those men who have died in the state of grace, but who have to make up for venial sins or the punishment due to sin. They can do nothing for themselves. They must depend upon the faithful on earth or the saints in heaven to help them reach eternal rest as quickly as possible.

How can we help the poor souls in purgatory? The very best way is to have Masses offered for them. There are also other means by which we can help. For example, we can say the Prayer before a Crucifix after Holy Communion, recite the Rosary in the presence of the Blessed Sacrament, or make the Way of the Cross. During the month of November, especially the first eight days, we should remember the dead by visiting a cemetery and praying for the souls of those who have passed. From November 1–8, when we pray at a cemetery for the souls in purgatory, we may gain a plenary indulgence for them––given that we have the right intention and are fully detached from sin. Here is a beautiful prayer we may recite for the souls of the dead: "Eternal rest grant unto them O Lord and let perpetual light shine upon them. May their souls and the souls of all the faithful departed, through the mercy of God, rest in peace. Amen."

Although the Church, as a good and loving Mother, remembers the holy souls in purgatory in every Sacrifice of the Mass, on All Souls' Day she is especially generous to them. She allows each priest to offer three Masses.

You might ask, "Why should we pray for the poor souls?" We have already learned many reasons. Another is that our prayers for these holy souls strengthen our friendship with them. How important it is to have friends that are close to God, who in turn will pray for us when we are in purgatory.

The Solemnity of Our Lord Jesus Christ, King of the Universe

On the last day of the liturgical year (ordinary form), we celebrate the Solemnity of our Lord Jesus Christ, King of the Universe. (In the extraordinary form, this feast is celebrated on the last Sunday in October.) During the whole liturgical year the Church reminds us of the Kingship of Christ. Every morning in the first hour of the Divine Office we pray: "Honor and glory through endless ages to the king of all ages. . . ." Every Collect in the Mass ends with the words "who lives and reigns forever." However, on the Feast of Christ the King we honor Him in a special way.

Jesus Christ is the divine King who "sits at the right hand of the Father" and shall return at the end of the world "to judge the living and the dead." He is the real King of heaven and earth, and of all living things. He rules over all men.

The Divine Office on this day pictures Christ as the King of peace. It also emphasizes over and over again that the kingdom of Christ shall last forever, and that all other rulers are subject to Christ. "He shall be called the Peaceful. . . His kingdom is an everlasting kingdom and all kings shall serve him and obey him."

Christ is God, the Creator and Redeemer of the whole human race; He is the Head of the Mystical Body: "He is the image of the invisible God . . . in him were created all things . . . He is before all creatures, and in him all things hold together" (Col. 1:15–17). Could you paint a more magnificent picture of Christ the King than this? Christ's mission on earth was to give back to man the divine life that was lost by our first parents.

Do you remember how Jesus, just before He was crucified, was taken before Pontius Pilate? The soldiers had told Pilate that Jesus said He was a King. Pilate then asked, "You are then a

king?" and Jesus replied: "I am a king. This is why I was born, and why I have come into the world" (Jn. 18:37).

On this day the Church asks us to show our love, gratitude, and loyalty to Christ the King of kings by giving up our wills to do His will. We are asked to offer ourselves to Him at the Sacrifice of the Altar.

When you receive Holy Communion on the Feast of Christ the King, tell Jesus that you know He is our King. Promise to do some little sacrifice to make up for the sins committed by those who refuse to recognize the Kingship of Christ. With the Solemnity of our Lord Jesus Christ, King of the Universe, we are completing the study of the liturgy. The liturgy, as you learned, is Christ: King, Priest, and Victim, at His great priestly work in the Mystical Body—His work of offering Himself in adoration to God and of bringing salvation to man. If we join with Christ in this work, we honor God, help our neighbor, and make certain of our eternal life in heaven.

When you learn to do something, you want to do it many times over so that you really know how to do it well. This year you have learned about the liturgy, and we hope you tried to live it in your daily life. Now, you ought to continue to practice it all through your life because living the liturgy, you know, means *living* with Christ, and in Christ, and like Christ.

FOR ME TO REVIEW

Catechism Lesson

21. Q. Is there but one God?

A. Yes; there is but one God.

22. Q. Why can there be but one God?

A. There can be but one God, because God, being supreme and infinite, cannot have an equal.

23. Q. How many Persons are there in God?

A. In God there are three Divine Persons, really distinct, and equal in all things—the Father, the Son, and the Holy Spirit.

27. Q. What do you mean by the Blessed Trinity?

A. By the Blessed Trinity I mean one God in three Divine Persons.

115. Q. **What is the Church?**
A. The Church is the congregation of all those who profess the faith of Christ, partake of the same sacraments, and are governed by their lawful pastors under one visible Head.

120. Q. **Why did Christ found the Church?**
A. Christ founded the Church to teach, govern, sanctify, and save all men.

114. Q. **Which are the means instituted by our Lord to enable men at all times to share in the fruits of the Redemption?**
A. The means instituted by our Lord to enable men at all times to share in the fruits of His Redemption are the Church and the sacraments.

119. Q. **Who are the successors of the other Apostles?**
A. The successors of the other Apostles are the bishops of the Holy Catholic Church.

244. Q. **Did anything remain of the bread and wine after their substance had been changed into the substance of the Body and Blood of our Lord?**
A. After the substance of the bread and wine had been changed into the substance of the Body and Blood of our Lord there remained only the appearances of bread and Wine.

245. Q. **What do you mean by the appearances of bread and wine?**
A. By the appearances of bread and wine I mean the figure, the color, the taste, and whatever appears to the senses.

Questions

1. Who is the Holy Spirit?
2. What effect did the Holy Spirit have upon the Apostles?
3. Why is Pentecost sometimes called "Whitsunday"?
4. What great mysteries of our faith do we recall on the Feast of the Blessed Trinity?
5. What does "Corpus Christi" mean?
6. Explain the sentence: By receiving the Holy Eucharist we become more closely united to Christ and to the members of the Mystical Body.
7. The Feast of the Sacred Heart is the feast of the love of Jesus. Explain this statement.
8. What do we mean when we say that the Blessed Virgin was assumed into heaven?
9. Humility and purity are the chief virtues of our Lady. Discuss ways in which we can imitate her in these two virtues.
10. Summarize the chief teachings of the Church which we learn from the liturgy.
11. Show how, by living with Christ and His Church in the liturgy, we become more like Christ in all His actions: kind, helpful, considerate, patient, modest, truthful, courageous, obedient, humble.

FOR ME TO REMEMBER

1. Ordinary Time is the longest period of the Liturgical Year.
2. The Blessed Trinity works in us through the sacraments.
3. The Feast of Corpus Christi is a solemn act of faith in the real presence of Christ in the Holy Eucharist.

4. The Feast of the Sacred Heart is often called the feast of the love of Christ. It is celebrated on the Friday of the week after the Feast of Corpus Christi.

5. St. Peter and St. Paul were great Apostles, chosen to do the work of Our Lord after His ascension into heaven. St. Paul is called the Apostle of the Gentiles.

7. Three great feasts of our Lady which come during the summer months are:
   - The Visitation of the Blessed Virgin Mary, May 31 (ordinary form) July 2 (extraordinary form)
   - Assumption of Our Lady, August 15
   - Immaculate Heart of Mary, Saturday after the Sacred Heart (ordinary form) August 22 (extraordinary form)

8. All Saints' Day and All Souls' Day are special feasts of the Mystical Body of Christ. On All Saints' Day we rejoice with all the holy souls in heaven and get a glimpse of what awaits us in heaven. On All Souls' Day we pray and mourn with the poor souls in purgatory, who are waiting to be freed from their sufferings.

9. On the Solemnity of our Lord Jesus Christ, King of the Universe, we show our love, gratitude, and loyalty to the divine King of heaven and earth.

FOR ME TO DO

1. Arrange a bulletin board showing important feasts which come during the summer months.

2. Learn and recite the *Magnificat.*

3. List some examples of virtues practiced by our Lady. Give practical examples of how they can be imitated.

4. Dramatize the scene of the *Visitation of Our Lady.*
5. Explain how the various members of the Mystical Body of Christ can help one another.
6. Try to attend Mass as often as you can and say a special prayer for the souls in purgatory.
7. Read the life of your patron saint. Tell the class some of the more outstanding things in the life of your patron.
8. Make simple costumes that a saint wore, or symbols that belong to him. Describe the life of each saint briefly.

Summary of Unit 6

Ten days after the Ascension of our Lord we celebrate the Feast of Pentecost. Pentecost marks the birthday of the Church because the Holy Spirit fully prepared the Church for her great work on earth, namely, the sanctification of men. To this day this work is being carried on in the Church, especially through the Holy Sacrifice of the Mass and the sacraments.

Ordinary Time is the longest period of the Liturgical Year. It extends to the beginning of Advent. The readings for the Sundays call our attention to Christ's teachings and His miracles. They remind us how to lead a good Christian life in union with Christ.

During the period after Pentecost, we celebrate many important feast days in honor of our Lord, the Blessed Virgin Mary, and the saints. Among them we especially remember the following: the feast of the Blessed Trinity, the feast of Corpus Christi, the feast of Saints Peter and Paul, the Visitation of the Blessed Virgin Mary, All Saints' Day, All Souls' Day, and the solemnity of our Lord Jesus Christ, King of the Universe.

Conclusion

We have spent this whole year studying the liturgy. We have learned that the liturgy is Christ the God-Man, our High Priest and King, offering Himself to God as our Victim:

Offering Himself for us and with us, as Head of His Mystical Body, of which we are the members.

Offering the divine sacrifice once offered on Calvary and now renewed on our altars.

Offering it to adore God in His greatness and to thank Him for His goodness, to atone for sin and, through that sacrifice and by means of His action in the sacraments and the other instruments of the liturgy, to gain for us the grace and strength we need to lead a life on earth modeled after the life of Christ our Lord and Savior.

In the liturgy, Christ in His Church lives through His life again so that we can live it with Him, so that we can live on earth as other Christs adoring God, atoning for sins, working for the salvation of mankind. May we all through the rest of our lives live year by year with Christ in the mysteries of the liturgy.

Write your answers on a separate sheet of paper

Part 1 Matching

Match each item in Column A with an item in Column B.

COLUMN A	COLUMN B
1. Beatitudes	A. Converted over 3000 on Pentecost
2. All Saints' Day	B. One God in three divine Persons
3. Blessed Trinity	C. The feast in which we celebrate the goodness of Christ in leaving us His Body and Blood to be our food and drink
4. St. Peter	D. The Feast of the Assumption of the Blessed Virgin Mary
5. Feast of the Sacred Heart	E. Composed the liturgy for the Feast of Corpus Christi
6. Corpus Christi	F. Reminds us of Christ's great love for us and His desire that we love Him in return.
7. Liturgy	G. Steppingstones to heaven
8. St. Thomas Aquinas	H. Honors saints in heaven
9. August 15	I. The Apostle of the Gentiles
10. St. Paul	J. Christ's priestly work in the Mystical Body

Part 2 Arrange in Order

Arrange these feasts or seasons in correct order by numbering the items 1 to 5 according to their proper place in the Liturgical Year.

A. Lent
B. Epiphany
C. Pentecost
D. Advent
E. Easter

Part 3 Yes or No

Read each question carefully. Then answer Yes or No.

1. Is Easter Sunday the birthday of the Church?
2. Do the gifts of the Holy Spirit make us more eager to do the will of God?
3. Does the Holy Spirit sanctify us through the gift of grace?
4. Do the Gospels for the Sundays after Pentecost remind us of Christ's sufferings?
5. Is the *Sign of the Cross* an act of faith in the three divine Persons?
6. Are the beatitudes good rules of conduct for forming a perfect Christian character?
7. Is loving others for the love of Jesus the best way for showing our love and gratitude to the Sacred Heart?
8. Does the study of liturgy help us to become more Christlike and Marylike?
9. Are the readings of the Mass guides to help us become more like Christ in our everyday actions, thoughts, and words?
10. Did St. Paul become the Head of the Church after St. Peter died?

Prayers

The Sign of the Cross

In the name of the Father, and of the Son, and of the Holy Spirit. Amen.

The Lord's Prayer

Our Father who art in heaven, hallowed be Thy name; Thy kingdom come; Thy will be done on earth as it is in heaven. Give us this day our daily bread; and forgive us our trespasses as we forgive those who trespass against us; and lead us not into temptation, but deliver us from evil. Amen.

The Hail Mary

Hail Mary, full of grace, the Lord is with thee; blessed art thou among women, and blessed is the fruit of thy womb, Jesus. Holy Mary, Mother of God, pray for us sinners, now and at the hour of our death. Amen.

Glory Be to the Father

Glory be to the Father, and to the Son, and to the Holy Spirit. As it was in the beginning, is now, and ever shall be, world without end. Amen.

The Apostles' Creed

I believe in God, the Father Almighty, Creator of heaven and earth; and in Jesus Christ, His only Son, Our Lord; who was conceived by the Holy Spirit, born of the Virgin Mary, suffered under Pontius Pilate, was crucified, died, and was buried. He descended into hell; the third day He arose again from the dead; He ascended into heaven, and sits at the right hand of God, the Father Almighty; from thence He shall come to judge the living and the dead. I believe in the Holy Spirit, the Holy Catholic Church, the communion of saints, the forgiveness of sins, the resurrection of the body, and life everlasting. Amen.

The Confiteor

Ordinary Form

I confess to almighty God
and to you, my brothers and sisters,
that I have greatly sinned
in my thoughts and in my words,
in what I have done,
and in what I have failed to do;
through my fault, through my fault,
through my most grievous fault;
therefore I ask blessed Mary ever-Virgin,
all the Angels and Saints,
and you, my brothers and sisters,
to pray for me to the Lord our God. Amen

Extraordinary Form

I confess to Almighty God,
to blessed Mary ever Virgin,
blessed Michael the Archangel,
blessed John the Baptist,
the holy Apostles Peter and Paul,
and to all the saints
that I have sinned exceedingly
in thought, word, and deed,
through my fault,
through my fault,
through my most grievous fault.
Therefore, I beseech blessed Mary ever Virgin,
blessed Michael the Archangel,
blessed John the Baptist,
the holy Apostles Peter and Paul,
and all the saints,
to pray for me to the Lord our God. Amen.

Morning Offering

O Jesus, through the Immaculate Heart of Mary, I offer Thee my prayers, works, joys and sufferings of this day for all the intentions of Thy Sacred Heart, in union with the Holy Sacrifice of the Mass throughout the world, in reparation for my sins, for the intentions of all our relatives and friends, and in particular for the intentions of the Hold Father. Amen.

The Angelus

V. The angel of the Lord declared unto Mary.
R. And she conceived of the Holy Spirit.

Hail Mary, full of grace! the Lord is with thee; blessed art thou among women, and blessed is the fruit of thy womb, Jesus. Holy Mary, Mother of God, pray for us sinners, now and at the hour of our death. Amen.

V. Behold the handmaid of the Lord.
R. Be it done unto me according to thy word.

Hail Mary, etc.

V. And the Word was made flesh.
R. And dwelt among us.

Hail Mary, etc.

V. Pray for us, O holy Mother of God.
R. That we may be made worthy of the promises of Christ.

Let Us Pray
Pour forth, we beseech Thee, O Lord, Thy grace into our hearts, that we to whom the Incarnation of Christ, Thy Son, was made known by the message of an angel, may by His passion and cross be brought to the glory of His resurrection, through the same Christ Our Lord. Amen.

Regina Coeli

(Said during Eastertide, instead of the Angelus)

Queen of heaven, rejoice, Alleluia.
For He whom thou didst deserve to bear, Alleluia.
Hath risen as He said, Alleluia.
Pray for us to God, Alleluia.
V. Rejoice and be glad, O Virgin Mary! Alleluia.
R. Because Our Lord is truly risen, Alleluia.

Let Us Pray
O God, who by the resurrection of Thy Son, Our Lord Jesus Christ, have vouchsafed to make glad the whole world, grant, we beseech Thee, that, through the intercession of the Virgin Mary, His Mother, we may attain the joys of eternal life. Through the same Christ Our Lord. Amen.

Hail, Holy Queen

Hail, Holy Queen, Mother of Mercy; hail, our life, our sweetness, and our hope! To thee do we cry, poor banished children of Eve; to thee we do send up our sighs, mourning and weeping in this vale of tears. Turn, then, most gracious advocate, thine eyes of mercy toward us; and after this our exile, show unto us the blessed fruit of thy womb, Jesus. O clement, O loving, O sweet Virgin Mary!

An Act of Faith

O my God, I firmly believe that Thou art one God in three Divine Persons, Father, Son, and Holy Spirit; I believe that Thy Divine Son became man, and died for our sins, and that He will come to judge the living and the dead. I believe these and all the truths which the Holy Catholic Church teaches, because Thou hast revealed them, who canst neither deceive nor be deceived.

An Act of Hope

O my God, relying on Thy almighty power and infinite mercy and promises, I hope to obtain pardon of my sins, the help of Thy grace, and life everlasting, through the merits of Jesus Christ, my Lord and Redeemer.

An Act of Love

O my God, I love Thee above all things, with my whole heart and soul, because Thou art all-good and worthy of all love. I love my neighbor as myself for the love of Thee. I forgive all who have injured me, and ask pardon of all whom I have injured.

An Act of Contrition

O my God, I am heartily sorry for having offended Thee, and I detest all my sins, because of Thy just punishments, but most of all because they offend Thee, my God, who art all-good and deserving of all my love. I firmly resolve, with the help of Thy grace, to sin no more and to avoid the near occasions of sin.

The Blessing Before Meals

Bless us, O Lord, and these Thy gifts, which we are about to receive from Thy bounty, through Christ Our Lord. Amen.

Grace After Meals

We give Thee thanks for all Thy benefits, O Almighty God, who livest and reignest forever; and may the souls of the faithful departed, through the mercy of God, rest in peace. Amen.

The Mysteries of the Rosary

The Five Joyful Mysteries

1. The Annunciation
2. The Visitation
3. The Birth of Our Lord
4. The Presentation of Our Lord in the Temple
5. The Finding of Our Lord in the Temple

The Five Luminous Mysteries

1. The Baptism of Our Lord in the Jordan
2. The Wedding Feast at Cana
3. Our Lord's Proclamation of the Kingdom of God
4. The Transfiguration of Our Lord
5. The Institution of the Eucharist

The Five Sorrowful Mysteries

1. The Agony of Our Lord in the Garden
2. The Scourging at the Pillar
3. The Crowning With Thorns
4. The Carrying of the Cross
5. The Crucifixion and Death of Our Lord

The Five Glorious Mysteries

1. The Resurrection of Our Lord
2. The Ascension of Our Lord into Heaven
3. The Descent of the Holy Spirit Upon the Apostles
4. The Assumption of Our Blessed Mother into Heaven
5. The Coronation of Our Blessed Mother in Heaven

The Immaculate Conception with the Fifteen Mysteries of the Rosary

Answer Key

Unit 1

Chapter 1

1. God
2. God is the Supreme Being
3. All good, true, powerful, wise, all-perfect
4. Man is a creature composed of body and soul and made in the image and likeness of God.
5. God made man to share His goodness with us.
6. Adam and Eve
7. He banished them from paradise.

Chapter 2

1. God the Son, the Second Person of the Trinity, the Redeemer
2. Jesus obeyed perfectly
3. Holy people who came before Jesus who foretold the coming of Christ
4. St. John the Baptist told people to prepare their hearts and to be sorry for their sins and do penance.
5. Nativity, Presentation, Passion and Death, Resurrection and Ascension.
6. That he was truly God
7. St. Peter

Chapter 3

1. Pentecost
2. Tongues of flame appeared above their heads, they were filled with the Holy Spirit, and they had the gift of tongues
3. Pentecost

Chapter 4

1. The faithful on earth, the blessed in heaven, and the souls in purgatory with Christ as their Head.

2. Communion is the united congregation of all holy people in harmony. Saints are the holy people who rejoice in God's life.
3. Answers may vary.
4. Prayers, good works, and sacrifices
5. They can pray for us.
6. At the Ascension.
7. Regularly, but especially whenever we commit mortal sin.
8. The bodies of the faithful will rise from the grave beautiful and perfect on the last day.
9. So we can join God body and soul.
10. The eternal happiness of perfect communion with God in paradise.
11. The place of eternal suffering separate from God.
12. Where we atone for our sins to prepare the soul for heaven.

To Prove My Mastery

PART 1.

1. body, soul
2. immortal
3. know, love, serve
4. Redeemer
5. sanctifying grace
6. disobeyed
7. Creator
8. eternal
9. Catholic Church
10. St. John the Baptist
11. Resurrection
12. St. Peter.
13. Communion of Saints
14. sharing or union
15. Easter Day

PART 2.

1. No
2. No
3. Yes
4. Yes
5. Yes
6. Yes
7. Yes
8. No
9. Yes
10. Yes
11. Yes
12. No

PART 3.

Group A
3 Jacob
1 Adam
2 Abraham
5 David
4 Juda

Group B
7 Ascension
3 Nativity
5 Passion and Death
2 Visitation
6 Resurrection
1 Annunciation
4 Presentation
8 Pentecost

Unit 2

Chapter 5

1. The Mystical Body of Christ
2. Jesus Christ
3. St. Peter
4. The Apostles
5. Because the body is seen and made of many parts, and it is mystical because it is supernatural, and the Church is of Christ.
6. Christ's teachings live in the Church today, Christ also lives in use through the sacraments, and Christ also lives through the Church today as the Mystical Body of the Church.
7. The Church has a different object than a normal club, its goal is heaven. Also, the Holy Spirit lives in the body of the Church.

Chapter 6

1. All who are baptized and profess the true faith.
2. Believe in Christ and the truths He revealed.
3. Trust in God as the giver of everlasting happiness in heaven.
4. Love of Christ and neighbor.
5. Through shared love, trust, and belief in Christ and His Church.
6. Answers may vary.

To Prove My Mastery

PART 1.

1. No
2. Yes
3. Yes
4. Yes
5. Yes
6. Yes
7. Yes
8. Yes

9. No
10. Yes

PART 2.

1. St. Peter
2. Pentecost
3. Jesus Christ
4. Charity
5. Bishops
6. Apostles, Church
7. Parable
8. Mystical Body
9. Jesus Christ
10. pope

Unit 3

Chapter 7

1. Liturgy means worship, this can take the form of adoration. Liturgy also means thanksgiving; the greatest thanksgiving is the Mass itself. Liturgy is begging God forgiveness, this can be found even in the Mass itself where we admit of our sins. There are many other possible answers.
2. Exterior worship is the worship we show through actions, like kneeling. Interior worship is the worship we do in our hearts. Interior worship is by far the greater of the two; it is the one which allows us to live with Christ.
3. Prayer is the interior worship; it is through prayer we grow closer to God. Christ prayed in the garden on Holy Thursday and Christ prayed on the cross.
4. In the Mass, Christ is the priest and the victim. In Baptism, Christ washes away the sins. It is Christ who forgives in confession. There are many other possible answers.

5. Through the sacraments and the liturgy, Christ transforms us to become more like Him.
6. The missal which contains the prayers and songs of the congregation at Mass. The Breviary which is used to recite the Divine Office. It shows which prayers and songs are to be used for the different days and liturgical seasons. The ritual is the book of prayers and rules for sacraments and blessings.

Chapter 8

1. Suffering to show love.
2. To act as a gift of love.
3. Priest, victim, and altar.
4. The bloody sacrifice requires a bloody victim, like the lambs, goats, and calves. An unbloody sacrifice is one which does not shed blood; the Last Supper and the Mass are unbloody sacrifices because the blood was shed for them at Calvary.
5. A bloody sacrifice.
6. An unbloody sacrifice.
7. The Mass is a real sacrifice: it has a priest, victim, and altar.
8. Jesus said the first Mass at the Last Supper in the Upper Room.
9. On Holy Thursday at the Last Supper.
10. We share in the sacrifice as part of the Mystical Body of Christ. Because of this we can offer ourselves together with Christ's sacrifice.
11. It is the high point and center of the Catholic faith. It is the sacrifice of God the Son, on Calvary, offered daily to the Father. It is the form of adoration most pleasing to God where the merits of the Redeemer are distributed to the faithful.

Chapter 9

1. The official daily prayers of the Church. It is Christ at prayer in His Church.
2. By praying the Divine Office, the faithful prepare themselves

for Holy Mass and receive the graces that flow from the liturgy. The Divine Office unites the faithful to Christ.
3. Psalm 22 (21)
4. King David
5. How to praise God.
6. Psalms are used in both and they are both made to adore God.

Chapter 10

1. Yes
2. Yes
3. Yes
4. Yes
5. Yes
6. Yes
7. Yes
8. Yes
9. Yes
10. Yes
11. Yes
12. Yes
13. Yes
14. Yes
15. Yes
16. No
17. Yes
18. No
19. Yes
20. Yes

Chapter 11

1. Blessed objects and holy things which help channel grace and help us prepare for grace.
2. The crucifix, the sign of the cross, and holy water.

3. The sacraments give grace directly, but sacramentals only help us to receive grace.
4. Christ through His Church.

Chapter 12

1. The year in the Church with its periods of time centered around the life of Christ, His mother and of the saints.
2. The first Sunday of Advent
3. Easter season
4. By living through His life in the liturgical calendar.
5. Offering ourselves with Him in grace throughout the year.
6. They both divide the year into seasons and they both focus on key events through holidays or holidays.

To Prove My Mastery

PART 1.

1. True
2. True
3. True
4. False
5. True
6. True
7. False
8. True

PART 2.

1. sanctifying grace
2. suffering
3. penance
4. Last Supper
5. sacramentals
6. Mass
7. missal
8. knowledge

9. Divine Office
10. psalms

PART 3.

1. A
2. B
3. A
4. A
5. C

PART 4.

1. G
2. F
3. I
4. A
5. J
6. C
7. B
8. D
9. E
10. H

Unit 4

Chapter 13

1. To redeem mankind and give everyone a way to join Him in heaven.
2. God foreshadowed sending redemption for all mankind through Christ by sending Adam and Eve clothes. God also promised them a Redeemer would be sent.
3. Holy people who came before Christ to proclaim His coming.
4. She teaches us that our hearts must be free from sin to receive Christ.
5. St. John the Baptist urges us to make straight the way of the

Lord.
6. Answers may vary.

Chapter 14

1. Coming
2. Four weeks
3. It is a time of preparation for Christ's coming.
4. St. Paul is telling us to wake up from our spiritual laziness which keeps us from God.
5. Because both prepare for Christ's coming.
6. She is our model for preparing for Christ and shows us how to choose to be holy.
7. Prepare people for Christ's coming. He was the precursor of Christ.
8. Because Christ came to redeem everyone since He makes us all brothers and sisters.
9. Because Christ's coming is near.
10. By receiving the sacraments especially Penance and Reconciliation.
11. The first line tells us the holes in our spiritual life will be filled. The second line says we must be Christ before everything else. The third line tells us we must bring our whole selves to God correcting our little crooked ways. The last line tells us that we must make our character more Christlike.
12. *Sapientia* - O Wisdom, *Adonai* - O Leader, *Radix Jesse* - O Root of Jesse, *Clavis David* - O Key of David, ***Oriens*** - O Orient, *Rex Gentium* - O King of Gentiles, *Emmanuel* - O God With Us.

Chapter 16

1.
   A. False
   B. True
   C. False

D. True
E. False
F. True
G. True

2.

A. prayer.
B. Father, Son
C. miracle
D. Holy Spirit
E. obedience
F. Gold
G. Divinity

To Prove My Mastery

PART 1.

Sentences will vary. Give credit for every sentence in which the words are used correctly.

PART 2.

1. A
2. C
3. A
4. B
5. C

PART 3.

1. Reverence for the Holy Name of Jesus.
2. We have been called to become members of the Mystical Body of Christ. Like the Magi we bring gifts to Christ when we are in the state of grace.
3. God is the ruler of the whole world, but He delegated some of His powers to our parents; therefore, we owe them love, respect, and obedience.
4. Through Baptism we are incorporated into the Mystical Body

of Christ. To remain as good members, we must "put on Christ." At His baptism, Jesus showed Himself to St. John and his followers. Today He shows Himself to people by living in us.

5. Emphasize the fact that Christ is the Redeemer of all men and that Christ is God. They remind us of Christ's divine power to work miracles.

Unit 5

Chapter 17

1.
   - A. Yes
   - B. Yes
   - C. No
   - D. Yes
   - E. Yes

2.
   - A. We wear ashes to remind us we are only dust and will return to dust.
   - B. The Palms from last year's Palm Sunday.
   - C. "Remember, you are dust and to dust you will return."
   - D. Every kind thought or deed adds treasure in heaven.
   - E. Because Lent is half over and Christ's resurrection is soon.
   - F. Flowers and rose colored vestments.

3.
   - A. 4.
   - B. 7.
   - C. 2.
   - D. 8.
   - E. 1.
   - F. 5.
   - G. 6.
   - H. 3.

Chapter 18

A. 2
B. 9
C. 4
D. 5
E. 8
F. 1
G. 7
H. 6
I. 3

To Prove My Mastery

PART 1.

1. C
2. A
3. B
4. A
5. B
6. B
7. D
8. C
9. C

PART 2.

1. F
2. T
3. T
4. T
5. T
6. F
7. T

PART 3.

1. Ash Wednesday
2. Laetare Sunday
3. Palm Sunday
4. Holy Thursday
5. Good Friday
6. Holy Saturday
7. Easter
8. Ascension Thursday

Unit 6

Chapter 19

1. God, the Third Person of the Trinity, the Paraclete
2. It gave them grace, made them brave, and helped them convert a great number of people.
3. It is from the practice of giving baptism on the vigil of that day and the white robes worn at Mass.
4. That God is Three Persons in One God, or One God in three Divine Persons.
5. Body of Christ.
6. By receiving and eating the Eucharist, we become one with Christ along with His Mystical Body, the Church.
7. It is the feast we celebrate the mercy and love which pours from Jesus' heart.
8. Mary was taken body and soul into heaven.
9. Answers may vary.
10. The liturgy teaches us how to live like Christ, with Christ, and in Christ.
11. Answers may vary.

To Prove My Mastery

PART 1.

1. G
2. H
3. B
4. A
5. F
6. C
7. J
8. E
9. D
10. I

PART 2.

1. Advent
2. Epiphany
3. Easter
4. Pentecost

PART 3.

1. No
2. Yes
3. Yes
4. No
5. Yes
6. Yes
7. Yes
8. Yes
9. Yes
10. No

Image Credits

cover The Last Supper (oil on panel), Macip, Vicente Juan (Juan de Juanes) (c.1510-79), Bridgeman Images
viii-1 God creating the sun, the moon and the stars in the Firmament, c.1650 (oil on copper), Brueghel, Jan the Younger (1601-78), photo © Christie's Images / Bridgeman Images
p3 Savaoph, God the Father, 1885-96 (oil on canvas), Vasnetsov, Victor Mikhailovich (1848-1926), Bridgeman Images
p4 The Creation of the World (oil on canvas), Le Sueur, Eustache (1617-55) / French, Bridgeman Images
p6 Eve tempted by the Serpent (colour litho), © Look and Learn / Bridgeman Images
p8 King David playing the harp (chromolitho), © Look and Learn / Bridgeman Images
p13 Jesus prays in the garden, illustration by Freedom Studio/Shutterstock
p15 Divine Mercy of Jesus Christ, illustration by Prasad K B/Shutterstock
p17 La Nativite De Notre Seigneur, Peinture murale d'apres Hipp Flandrin, St Germain des Pres, a Paris (chromolitho), © Look and Learn / Bridgeman Images
p19 "He is Risen" (colour litho), © Look and Learn / Bridgeman Images
p21 The Baptism of Christ (gouache on paper), © Look and Learn / Bridgeman Images
p23 Pentecost, 1732 (oil on canvas), Restout, Jean II (1692-1768), Bridgeman Images
p25 Pentecost II, F. Maino, Restored Traditions
p27 The Forerunners of Christ with Saints and Martyrs, 1423-24 (egg tempera on wood), Angelico, Fra (Guido di Pietro/Giovanni da Fiesole) (c.1387-1455), Bridgeman Images
p29 Eastern Black Swallowtail Caterpillar's pupate, photo by IrinaK/ Shutterstock
p36-37 Disputa, from the Stanza della Segnatura, 1508-11 (fresco), Raphael (Raffaello Sanzio of Urbino) (1483-1520), Bridgeman Images
p41 Giving of the Keys to St. Peter, from the Sistine Chapel, 1481 (fresco), Perugino, Pietro (c.1445-1523), Bridgeman Images
p44 The Transfiguration (oil on panel), Raphael (Raffaello Sanzio of Urbino) (1483-1520), Photo © Stefano Baldini / Bridgeman Images
p49 Allegorie de la vigne (engraving), © Look and Learn / Bridgeman Images
p58-59 The Resurrection, 15th century (tempera on panel), Master of the Osservanza, (fl.c.1436), Founders Society Purchase / Gift of Mr & Mrs Henry Ford II / Bridgeman Images
p62 Mass in the Catholic Church, photo by Cavee/Shutterstock
p71 Chalice and ciborium on the altar during the traditional Latin Mass, photo by Thoom/Shutterstock
p73 Christ on the Cross, 1884 (oil on canvas), Munkacsy, Mihaly (1844-1900), Bridgeman Images
p76 Hands of Catholic priest on altar, photo by Calamity Jane/Shutterstock
p81 Family praying in church, photo by Rawpixel.com/Shutterstock
p83 Ancient statue of king David from facade of St. Jacques church in Brussels,

Belgium, photo by De Jongh Photography/Shutterstock
p86 Holy host in the hands of the priest, photo by wideonet/Shutterstock
p88 Baptism ceremony in Catholic Church, photo by sweet marshmallow/Shutterstock
p92 Golden monstrance, photo by MARI TERE/Shutterstock
p95 Bride and groom during the wedding ceremony, photo by Art_man/Shutterstock
p103 Christian medals, Saint-Gervais, France, Godong / Bridgeman Images
p109 Light a pink candle on the Advent wreath, photo by Roza Sharipova/Shutterstock
p115 Victorian greeting card of an angel and two children praying, c. 1880 (colour litho), Photo © David Pearson / Bridgeman Images
p119 Priest saying the extraordinary form, traditional Latin Catholic mass, photo by Thoom/Shutterstock
p120-121 Adoration of the Magi detail, 1423 (tempera on panel), Fabriano, Gentile da (c.1370-1427), Photo © Raffaello Bencini / Bridgeman Images
p123 God Clothing Adam and Eve, from a book of Bible Pictures, c.1250 (vellum), Brailes, William de (fl.c.1230), Bridgeman Images
p124 Isaiah (engraving), © Look and Learn / Bridgeman Images
p126-127 Annunciation, 1472-75 (oil on panel) (post restoration), Vinci, Leonardo da (1452-1519), Photo © Raffaello Bencini / Bridgeman Images
p131 Advent Wreath, photo by Derek Hatfield/Shutterstock
p136 The Immaculate Conception (oil on canvas), Sassoferrato, Il (Giovanni Battista Salvi) (1609-85), Photo © Christie's Images / Bridgeman Images
p140 John the Baptist, Copping, Harold (1863-1932), © Look and Learn / Bridgeman Images
p143 Decorative pink wax candle, photo by New Africa/Shutterstock
p147 The Adoration of the Shepherds, 1622 (oil on canvas), Honthorst, Gerrit van (1590-1656), Artothek / Bridgeman Images
p157 The infant Jesus, © Look and Learn / Bridgeman Images
p159 Christmas celebration (photo), Godong/UIG / Bridgeman Images
p166 The Stoning of Stephen, © Look and Learn / Bridgeman Images
p167 Saint John (engraving), Robida, Albert (1848-1926), © Look and Learn / Bridgeman Images
p170 The Holy Family by J. Palinka, Restored Traditions
p172 Adoration of the Magi, 1857 (oil on card), Flandrin, Hippolyte (1809-64), Bridgeman Images
p176 The Presentation in the Temple (oil on canvas), Bourdon, Sebastien (1616-71), Bridgeman Images
p184-185 The Resurrection, c.1715-16 (oil on canvas), Ricci, Sebastiano (1658-1734), © Dulwich Picture Gallery / Bridgeman Images
p187 Christ in the Wilderness, 1873 (oil on canvas), Kramskoy, Ivan Nikolaevich (1837-87), Sputnik / Bridgeman Images
p189 Cross made of ashes, photo by Thoom/Shutterstock
p191 Woman with cross on forehead, photo by berni0004/Shutterstock
p194 Jesus in the desert, subjected to the temptation of the devil, Dore, Gustave (1832-83), Stefano Bianchetti / Bridgeman Images
p197 Group of kids playing tug-of-war, photo by Veronica Louro/Shutterstock
p201 Easter week (photo), Godong/UIG / Bridgeman Images
p202 Palm leaf, photo by Dewin ID/Shutterstock

p204 The Last Supper (oil on panel), Macip, Vicente Juan (Juan de Juanes) (c.1510-79), Bridgeman Images
p206 The angel giving Jesus strength during his Agony in the Garden of Gethsemane (colour litho), © Look and Learn / Bridgeman Images
p208 Crucifix, photo by GrahamMoore999/Shutterstock
p209 The burial of Jesus (colour litho), © Look and Learn / Bridgeman Images
p221 The Resurrection, right hand predella panel from the Altarpiece of St. Zeno of Verona, 1456-60 (oil on panel), Mantegna, Andrea (1431-1506), Bridgeman Images
p224 Saint Faustina Kowalska, Photo © CCI / Bridgeman Images
p225 Sacred Heart of Jesus, illustration by Petr812/Shutterstock
p226 The disciples encounter Jesus on the road to Emmaus (engraving), Gustave Dore. Photo by Nicku/Shutterstock
p229 Statue of Jesus Christ Good Shepherd, photo by Zwiebackesser/Shutterstock
p230 The Resurrection of Christ, c.1502 (oil on panel), Raphael (Raffaello Sanzio of Urbino) (1483-1520), Bridgeman Images
p235 The Ascension, c.1305 (fresco), Giotto (Giotto di Bondone) (c.1266-1337), Bridgeman Images
p243 The Virgin and Child (The Madonna of the Book), Sandro Botticelli (1445-1510), public domain via Wikimedia Commons
p244-245 Pentecost, 1732 (oil on canvas), Restout, Jean II (1692-1768), Bridgeman Images
p246 Holy Spirit symbol, illustration by Thoom/Shutterstock
p248 The Pentecoot Back of the Maesta altarpiece, 1308-1311 (tempera on panel), Duccio di Buoninsegna, (c.1278-1318), Luisa Ricciarini / Bridgeman Images
p253 Feast of Corpus Christi, from Preces Variae, c.1500 (gouache & bodycolour on vellum), Bridgeman Images
p256 Jesus appearing to Saint Margaret Mary (Margaret Mary) Alacoque (1647-1690) mystical of the Order of Mosaic Visitation. St. Peter's Basilica in Rome (Vaticano, San Pietro), Luisa Ricciarini / Bridgeman Images
p258 Immaculate heart of Mary statue, photo by Immaculate/Shutterstock
p261 Detail of statue of St Peter in front of St Peters basilica, Vatican, Rome, Italy, photo by Martin M303/Shutterstock
p262 Statue of St. Paul outside the basilica of St. Peter, photo by nomadFra/Shutterstock
p265 Assumption of the Virgin, Francesco Botticini (1446–1498), public domain via Wikimedia Commons
p271 Triptych of Earthly Vanity and Divine Salvation, Christ in Glory from the reverse of the central panel, c.1485 (oil on panel), Memling, Hans (c.1433-94), Bridgeman Images
p280 The Virgin in Prayer, 1640-50 (oil on canvas), Sassoferrato, Il (Giovanni Battista Salvi) (1609-85), Bridgeman Images
p287 The Immaculate Conception with the Fifteen Mysteries of the Rosary (oil on canvas), Cabrera, Miguel (1695-1768), Photo © Christie's Images / Bridgeman Images
p288 Interior of a Scriptorium, School of Segovia (oil on panel), Bridgeman Images